THE CHRONICLES OF SYNCHRONICITY

Copyright © 2019 by Kimberely Stanworth (Kays)
First Edition – 2019

All rights reserved.

No part of this publication may be reproduced in any form, or by any means, electronic or mechanical, including photocopying, recording, or any information browsong, storage, or retrieval system, without permission in writing from The Ingram Book Company or Kimberley Stanworth (Kays).

ISBN
Paperback – 978-1-7770537-0-3
Hardcover – 978-1-7770537-1-0
Digital Edition – 978-1-7770537-2-7
Audiobook – 978-1-7770537-3-4

1. BODY, MIND & SPIRIT, INSPIRATION & PERSONAL GROWTH
2. FANTASY - CONTEMPORARY
3. SELF HELP - SPIRITUALITY

Distributed to the trade by The Ingram Book Company

THE CHRONICLES OF
SYNCHRONICITY

∞

WHITE IS NOT ALWAYS LIGHT;
BLACK IS NOT ALWAYS DARK.

A Spritual Fantasy Through The Sacred Journey of Kate and Ethan.

BY
KIM KAYS

May your heart be forever inspired by the sacred synchronicities that flow through your world. You are loved.

Contents

The Dark Night of the Soul • 1

When We Lived in a Tribe • 13

The Sylvethian Realm • 27

Evia And Elias Find One Another • 41

Kate and Ethan Synchronistically Meet • 53

The Ayahuasca Journey • 65

New Beginnings, New Perspectives • 81

The Journey to The Sun • 93

Social Struggles and Healing Visions • 105

Energy Healing Practises • 117

A Rite of Passage • 129

Dream Work • 141

A Sun Dance Birthday • 151

Space of Love • 163

The Wedding • 177

The Journey To My Future Self • 187

Elemental Portals • 197

A Light Story of Humanity • 207

ACKNOWLEDGMENTS

This book is dedicated to all of you sweet souls out there who are looking for answers. Synchronicity Squad, you know who you are.

It is also dedicated to the many people who helped me along my own journey, I would not be where I am today if it were not for your grace and kindness.

Finally, I dedicate this book to the love of my life, Eddie. Many chapters are based on our interactions together.

EDITORS NOTE

This story is written from the perspective of a woman reflecting over her life. There are moments where the voice is being spoken from either her past, present, or future self, or in reflection of a vision.

ONE

The Dark Night of the Soul

∞

MY NAME IS Kate, and this is the unforgettable story of my awakening to Life and to Synchronicity. Thinking back over my life so far, I realize my experiences up until this point have all woven together to create a magnificent tapestry. This elegant tapestry has been interlaced with both dark and light thread, and every colour in-between. Though my story is not yet complete, many lengths of its' thread have secretly stitched themselves together, forming a tale all their own. It is a never-ending story that is continuously being woven by the Chronicles (i.e., stories through time) of Synchronicity. These threads reach out into the infinite galaxy of possibilities, and so do yours.

So, now is the time. Synchronicity has called me to share this story so that it may be of value to those who need to receive it the most. It's a story that few would have the courage to share—because it is so unconventional—but share I will, nonetheless. Let me begin by telling you a story of my darkest night—a night I now understand to be the gateway of my soul's awakening. To get there, I will transport you through time to when I was comfortable enough to face the repressed emotions still lingering from the earlier ordeal. My narrative begins a year later, on an unsuspecting rainy evening, wherein my remembering and revelations of this unusual event begin to appear.

• • •

One drizzly evening, as I settle into my comfy, warm bed, gratitude fills my being. I ponder over some of the most recent, unlikely events, and replay the synchronicities in my mind. I had stumbled upon an opportunity to travel to several countries through some job opportunities. I was especially eager yet apprehensive to be starting such an extraordinary journey. After all, I knew this was a blessing from Synchronicity, which would take me even closer to my 'true' path, or so I hoped. As the rain began to pelt favourably against my bedroom window, outside of my little house in England, I melt into an unusual sense of tranquillity and accomplishment. I'm awash in the sudden, yet heart filling feeling that I am now at a place of deeper understanding in my life.

I still suffer many nights spent pondering over unsuccessful jobs and relationships that did not suit me. Yet, as if it was a passing illusion, none of the events of my past seemed to matter. Right now I could sense destiny calling—with my travelling adventures commencing tomorrow, a surge of excitement, paired with a healthy dose of anxiousness looms. There is distinct confidence in the flow and pull of the universe, beckoning me to keep moving forward into the unknown.

Holding this welcomed new feeling in my heart, I turn off my bedside lamp and gaze at the stars out of my window. Speculating thoughts overtook me again. How I had managed to swap the nine-to-five lifestyle with a ticket to travel the world instead? I made sense of this profound luck thanks to Synchronicity. The conscious awareness of life and unlikely coincidences which align for a deeper meaning and reason. I am still relatively new to this awareness of Synchronicity. It was only recently that I came across the notion that we are all active co-creators of our world. It had been revealed to me that the pairing of Synchronicity and spirituality could operate as the 'software'. Software that Source uses to align the dynamic resonance of our dreams, with the manifest reality of the world.

As I begin to relax into my body now, listening to the rain trickle and tickle the rooftops, I find myself drifting in and out of sleep. Simultaneously, the visions characteristic of this in-between state begin to emerge. With a new sense of alertness, my attention is directed toward a place that feels like home. Here, I can see and sense worlds within worlds of which, my conscious mind usually forgets about the next day. These nightly inner travels can traverse space and time, unhindered by the 'laws of physics'. Ordinarily, these journeys are into situations from my past, but also to visions of my potential future. Tonight, however, my intuition is guiding me to visit somewhere explicit.

Abruptly, with the unmistakable force of an outdated paradigm, I am jolted awake, unsettled by the quickened beat of my heart. My mind had been reminiscing over my discomforting past circumstances again. I suddenly felt dissolution, sensing into the fears that lay ahead of me, as well as the past that still haunted me. This last year had been filled with the most intense obscurity. So many changes and seeming mistakes had been made. It bothered me presently to know that the energy charge was mostly still alive in my heart. Even with these new opportunities now beckoning me forward, I still had a lot of shadows to face within.

Earlier in the year, I uncovered a social anxiety disorder, which had spurned my addiction to alcohol during most of my teenage years. Leaving me with a painful stomach ulcer and a great deal of inner confusion at the time. It got so bad that I was losing the will to live, and became severely depressed during the final months of writing my dissertation at university. I recognised that I had experienced so many fears of failure throughout my life. However, I had finally finished what I thought was impossible—graduating from university and finding a job. Yet, my path was now to leave all that behind to travel the world. Deep in my heart, I knew that the trials and tribulations were far from over, but a readiness came about after a challenging experience prior, which I will tell you about shortly.

I had already tried my hand at many jobs, including working in a call centre. To be candid, I hated every second of it. To keep myself motivated at the time, I created an online spiritual business in hopes that it would allow me to experience a deeper calling. What actually happened was even better. This new vocation began aligning me with valuable Synchronicities—the gravity of which I would not be fully aware of until years to come. The drudgery of the call centre was my idea of hell, and I only lasted five months there until resigning, even without knowing what on earth I would do next.

Quitting meant going back home again, to a sense of shame and the all-to-familiar lingering feeling of my unworthiness. Regardless, I realised my choice to get out of there was a far cry better than living in a cramped, cold, city house with three random strangers. I missed the countryside and nature. It was so far outside of my preferred way of life that I could feel the life force dwindling within me. Getting out of there was the single biggest decision that changed the course of my life. As I ponder all of this, I settle down again and readjust my sleeping position.

"It doesn't matter now, though," I quietly assert to myself, "I'm right where I need to be." The fear in my chest subsiding as I realise Synchronicity is on my side now. I'd been feeling it work its magic behind the scenes for a while now. I noticed new opportunities rewarding me every time I would gratefully flow with the divine timing of the universe. By seeking to venture out into an unknown world, a unique chance has perfectly lined up for me this time. In closing an old door, even without knowing what I would do next, a brand new door of opportunity and excitement has opened to me. This time though, I knew I had to make a choice to tap into my courage instead of fear.

Disregarding this, my mind suddenly argued: "But how do I not choose fear?" Anxiety and depression had been a part of my life for over a decade! At school, college, and work-life, everything had seemed backwards to me. No matter how hard I tried, I could not seem to fit in anywhere. A consistent feeling of inferiority had travelled with me throughout those younger years. This elusive rejection from life eventually led me to the desperation of continually coming home drunk at four am in the night, to then spend days with my head in the toilet. This had become a too regular occurrence for my soul, something had to change—and something did change.

"What was safe or spiritual about any of the aspects of the social world I grew up in?" A loud voice butted in again. I had tried it all, partying, studying, smoking, working, drinking, the usual stuff the 'cool kids' would do. I was so desperate to heal and find answers during my days at university. I visited doctors and began taking antidepressants. I even made the decision to try synthetic marijuana after a recommendation from a friend. The decision to try this foreign substance transformed my longing for answers into a Dark Night of the Soul. Let's back up several years ago to my final year as a student at university.

This dark night began on an ordinary evening alone in my room at university. After just three puffs of synthetic 'fake' marijuana, I experienced a crippling falling feeling all throughout my body. My consciousness plummeted into deep darkness, completely disorienting my senses. This incident was unlike anything I had ever experienced before. I mentally traversed something that would change my life forever this night. As I travel into this memory now, I'm reliving what it looked and felt like to sink deeper and deeper into the darkest layers of the Earth. During the experience, I could see each earthen layer, annihilating any sense of reality, as I plummeted below myself, into what felt like the depths of hell. That night alone, fearful and confused, something changed in me that was preparing me for a new future—but it came with a great deal of pain and suffering.

Reminiscing, I can clearly recall the reaction of my heart rapidly pulsating in my chest. It felt so intense that I feared I was about to pass out, and no one would be there to help me. At this notion, I fell into a full-blown panic attack, and eventually into an unconscious state—but not before experiencing some of the darkest shadows of my being. It was all so scary and disorientating. This journey into my own darkness felt like torture as I was immersed into every single life decision that I had ever made and later regretted. As I lay in this state of semi-unconsciousness, I felt numb and completely devoid of love. Lying here, pressing into the eeriness of this horrid experience had me shivering in my bed now. Thankfully, my higher self is simultaneously reminding me of the fact that this was all part of the transmutation and transformation process I was on.

When I finally came around from this hellish 'drug trip' years ago, I could hardly believe my eyes to be back in my same university bedroom. It was as though I was in some kind of video game, travelling back in time to view me from outside of myself. Everything seemed extremely bright and pierced my senses. Since the experience had been so traumatising, I felt the inmost sense of shame and confusion at the time. I remembered trying to ground, getting up from my bed and placing one foot at a time on the floor. Afterwards, I desperately searched my room for any small presence of love or hope. Anything that would help me make sense of what I had just gone through.

Rummaging through my books, as my head was still spinning uncontrollably, I found a photo album of my family that I had packed before going to university. As I looked at its pages, I saw the faces of my separated mother and father's faces. I looked deeply into the eyes of my family and all I could hear was a loud, disturbing voice in my head shouting, "There is no love here! Love doesn't exist! You're kidding yourself!" It was as though I had some kind of dementors all around me, yelling at me inside, whilst I tried to search for love.

After the drug trip, it felt like love had been drawn out of me, and now I felt utterly hopeless in trying to find it through pictures. The effects of this synthetic drug were still apparent, though these disturbing thoughts also showed me where my mindset was at the time. My untempered, unhindered, and deeply buried past had paved the way for such a negative experience to unfortunately occur. I realized that I had a lot of inner child healing to do. There were many experiences from my history that were coming to the surface to be healed, though I did not know this at the time.

Remembering all that accompanied this night, I can still feel the sensations of falling into a dark abyss of bleakness. The rest of this memory fades away into blurriness now. The last part I remember about this time in my life is the morning after from which I awoke from this nightmare experience. I remember how I knew, even at the time, that I was somehow stronger because of what had happened. It felt as though I had faced some of my darkest shadows, and had done so alone. I had been through the worst experience I had ever known and come out of it alive. No other experience compared to this Dark Night of the Soul, which could only mean I had hit rock bottom. Though, I had thankfully faced some of my fears and got to the other side. I had passed the test, and now, a whole year later, I simply had to process the emotions that came with it. After this past memory emerged, I fell into a deep sleep. Sensing that much healing progress had been made this night before my travels.

Whilst I am away with the fairies in dream space now, across the globe, Ethan is just waking up to start his day. To premise, I have not yet met Ethan at this point in my life. The reason I bring him up here is that he plays a pivotal role in my future. Even as early as two years before our meeting, Synchronicity is already connecting us together somehow, unbeknownst to us both. He is a dark and handsome looking chap, with radiant eyes that charismatically captivate anyone who looks into them. He was a few years older than Kate and a profoundly spiritual man who had been on the path of revelation for a long time.

It's six am as Ethan rolls out of bed and takes stock of his slumber. He notices an intense feeling come about as if he had been run over by a bus on this night. "What on earth did I dream about?" he wonders to himself. Prepping for the day, he gets dressed and psyches himself up for another working day—one filled with the trials and tribulations of selling products in a mall store. As he drives to work, he pleads with his angels, just as he does on his drive to work every morning. Only this time it felt as though someone new was listening. 'This cannot be all there is to my life, where do I go from here?' contemplating this question to himself. As he turns the corner, Ethan then notices the rising sun just above the trees and begins slowly counting his mala beads one by one, taking a deep breath with each bead. Gazing into the sun, he hears a voice in his head asking him, "What is your soul truly calling for?" to which Ethan replies, "Well, it certainly isn't to spend my days in a concrete box with no windows, day after day. There must be more that I am here to do in this life?!"

Unbeknownst to him, this is Ethan's last day working in sales. He finally had enough and decided it was time to move on from this tiresome job. He had no idea what was next, but miraculously, on his way out of the mall a kind fellow struck up a conversation with him. Ethan was much more equipped to allow Synchronicity to flow in his life. This coincidental conversation saved a night worth of worries as he was given a job that same week. As Ethan drove home from work that day, he heard the whispers of providence playing over in his mind again. He realized that in closing one door, a new door will always open. Even on the brink of one's own seeming destruction or extinction, sometimes the choice to move on is one of the bravest choices one could ever make. The divine timing of this breaking point, opens the door, each and every time, to something even more miraculous.

As dusk starts to appear in Canada, across the pond in England, the sun is casting its golden rays into Kate's bedroom. Subsequently, I did not remember much of what I had dreamt about the previous night. Though, I knew the reliving of my Dark Night of the Soul had helped to revive something. I felt lighter within my being, as though something had released from me. I hastily got ready for a day of travelling ahead as I was about to jump on a plane to visit family who lived abroad. Before starting my new adventure, I was planning to have a reunion in Tokyo.

Several hours later, and a fourteen-hour plane trip to Japan, my excitement seemed to vanish out of sight. I felt more triggered than ever by some of my families behaviours. After an evening spent together, we had a heated argument, and the same fearful voices in my head began to play again. I ran to the hotel I was staying at in tears, just several hours after getting off the plane. Still, I was unwilling to believe these loathsome thoughts that told me love did not exist. I remembered my previous night's trip down memory lane and recollected having I called my mother shortly after the terrible drug trip, to explain how I felt lost and depressed. The same isolation I felt back then was creeping up on me again. Having admitted to my depression, I felt isolated at being the only one seemingly facing this kind of turmoil in life. Staring blankly at the ceiling in my hotel room now, I tried to compute how I was feeling about it all—utterly lost and helpless again. Though for some miraculous reason, I had an instinct for the first time in my whole life, to ask angels for guidance. As I closed my watery eyes, I began to have a full-blown vision like no other.

This vision was a new phenomenon for me. Completely unlike anything I had experienced before, at least in this lifetime anyway. I relaxed and let go of the day's troubles and tensions. Then I saw through my imagination, that my whole body was now ascending into the clouds. Rising so high into the air, that even the sky was no longer blue, but a magnificent, shimmering colour of pink and white. I finally found myself laying on a comfortable table, floating on a cloud within this utopian looking paradise. This place looked familiar to me but completely otherworldly. It resembled an enormous, translucent sphere, that appeared to have edges until you got closer. This space was seemingly infinite, without boundaries or an end. I began to revel in the feelings of safety and security here, and suddenly I felt the presence of others there with me.

As I looked to the right of my vision, I saw the outline of a tall woman, clasping her hands together in prayer mudra. She was incredibly elegant and a brilliant white light poured from out of her robes. I recognised this woman somehow, and asked her, without hesitation, if she was my Guardian Angel. This Lightbeing smiled, "Yes, my love, and we have been waiting for you". I felt so encapsulated by her nurturing, motherly energy as she approached. Then I noticed another being out of the corner of my eye moving closer, he seemed to be somewhat wary of my reaction. I assured this man telepathically that I was not afraid. He came to me and stood by my side, clasping my hands tightly together. I felt a powerful, fatherly companionship with him, and breathed a sigh of relief as he kissed my forehead. A deep love stirred for them both in my heart. I embarked upon the idea that they were, in fact, my Spirit Guides.

A sincere sensation of love began to emerge and rise throughout my whole body now. Tingling my spine and cranium as the energy travelled throughout my being. My Lightbeing guides started to perform some Energy Healing on me, a type of advanced Reiki, I thought. Carefully guiding their hands over my chakras, they worked on each energy centre down the central line of my spine. I had never experienced anything so deeply blissful and tranquil in my whole life. When I awoke in my hotel room a few hours later, I felt incredibly grateful for the entire experience. It was the most magical gift of love and support. The least I could think to do was to write it all down, in order not to forget any of it.

THE CHRONICLES OF SYNCHRONICITY

TWO

When We Lived in a Tribe

∞

After what turns out to be a revelatory two weeks spent with my family, I am ready to take on a new adventure alone. This time, with a deeper trust in Synchronicity, since I will be alone. This trust is deeply rooted in the astonishing visions that continue to occur for me. A great sense of freedom and liberation occurs as I transit to the next country on my list, Austria. I leave the train at my last stop and stride down the central city of Vienna. The sun shines its rays of what feels like pure light on my whole being. Its radiance stands out to me more than any other, as though it was the first time the sun had ever smiled at me. I breathe in the fresh air of freedom. I was in this new city, alone and independent. The beauty and simplicity of life took hold of me in a new and exciting way.

There is a deep undercurrent of support to this whole place that I begin to remember now. It feels like a profound, subtle resonance that's here not just for me, but for everything in existence. While walking through the crowds and gazing up at the monumental museums and galleries before me, boundless energy carries within my being. My jovial attitude attracts the attention of a group of ticket scalpers, each promoting a local orchestra held nearby. One of them calls over to me, and as I engage in a conversation with him, I sense a great gift is about to be given to me. This friendly stranger invites me to attend an orchestra in a prestigious music hall across the way that very same night. I ask how much the ticket is and he tells me, "Free". I can hardly believe it and wonder whether I should accept this kind strangers offer.

I decided to take a risk and follow my gut instinct by going to meet the kind man that night. We happened to rendezvous next to a gigantic, rainbow water fountain. Mesmerised by this, I take lots of pictures of the fountain in every single one of its rainbow colours. I understand this night that there is a real sense of artistry to what city can behold at twilight. As we queue up towards the orchestra halls, I eagerly envisage the manifestations of exceptional experiences in my world recently. How my newfound positivity is allowing me to trust in the universe wholeheartedly. With these wonderful thoughts swimming around in my mind, I know I am about to experience a truly magical evening. Unexpectedly, within the city walls, which so often felt abhorrent to my idea of happiness.

The young gentlemen and I take our seats near the front row of the orchestra. I listen to this awe-inspiring music harmoniously vibrating from each instrument attentively. An overwhelming feeling begins to well up within me. As the night unfolds, I feel as though each musical note and each person is speaking to me personally. The sentiment is of deep reverence met with a sudden need to release tears of disbelief from within me. The music is so transcendental that it feels like only the melody and I exist in these marvellous moments. Gratitude does not entirely cover what I'm feeling during this experience. I'm overwhelmed with the joy for this gift from Grace and Synchronicity. After the show,

I once again thank the gentleman and bid farewell to this kind stranger with a full heart. As I ride the bus back to my hostel, a huge smile adorns my face. However, by the time I climb into my empty hostel room bed, my heart regresses into its weariness, from a deep sense of loneliness.

...

It has been several weeks into Ethan's new job now, and he has been willingly working from home. Having tailored his preferences to work within the field of health and wellness, he felt more self-assured than ever that he was on the right path. This welcomed new direction allowed Ethan to answer his souls' calling to assist people in the world of spiritual and physical health. As he stepped outside and sat in his garden on his lunch break, he smiled at the thought of manifesting a better path for himself in just a few days. Even so, looking around his environment and sensing into his being, something was seemingly missing. It was heavy loneliness that had been carried for many years. Instead of dwelling with it for too long, he decided to hand it over to the angels and release it to love.

For it is true love that he longed for within his heart the most, and he was willing to wait until the end of the world to find it. Ethan took an oath to himself that he would not settle for anything less than 'The One' from now on—even if it meant being alone for the rest of his life. As Ethan fell asleep to a romantic movie that night, someone met him energetically in his dreams, someone he was not expecting. These experiences all happened during the same time Kate was on a bike ride around the countryside near her hostel. She suddenly found herself beginning to envision something wondrously thrilling and exciting — the idea of meeting the man of her dreams.

Using her imagination, she allowed her whole being to flow

with the excitement of every emotion that was now arising. As she walked up the rocky hill towards the trees in the distance, she began to feel her whole body buzzing. Now fully immersed in the feelings of what it would be like meeting the love of her life. She climbed atop her bike again and began peddling with tremendous agility and stamina. Exploding with euphoria, and a sense of deep, warm, loving feelings in her being, she floated with the wind, feeling love pulse through her every cell as her soul gently whispered, "He is coming".

...

Sometime later, it was time to move on from Austria. I had discovered much about myself already — experienced trials and tribulations, and the ups and downs that came with this new independent lifestyle. I landed at my next destination after spending a miserable twenty-four hours travelling and rushed to the airport toilets to be sick. Yes, a new adventure awaited me. But this time it came with stomach-stirringly more anticipation and trepidation than the last journey! I was about to start a new job as a waitress, something I had never tried before. I had decided to join WWoofing accommodation for my next experience, which meant I would work in exchange for my accommodation and food. It's my first time doing something like this so far away from home. Even though I was trying to ignore my challenge with social anxiety, I was still, nonetheless, beyond nervous about meeting my new boss. Seemingly able to ignore these potent feelings, I stepped outside of the airport and breathed in the fresh air of New Zealand. As if to greet me with an outreaching hand, a momentous mountain stood before me. I breathed in a deep sense of astonishment and, somehow, a remembrance of this place like no other.

Over the next few months, and after some awkward starts, I

got to learn the role of working as a waitress. Although I had tried my best at waitressing, it did not seem good enough for my boss. Deep in my heart, I longed to see more of nature again. Every day I researched areas nearby that were part of the film 'The Lord of the Rings' so that I could fantasise about being close to the magic of the Elves and Ancient Lemuria. The work at the restaurant was long and hard, and it turned out I was merited in my anxiety about waitressing. Some unjust behaviour took place for me and the others during my time spent there. My boss was the kind of character who chose to behave in nothing short of verbal and psychological abuse toward his employees.

I'd never experienced this kind of vulnerability before, and in my naivete or perhaps strength, I just took it. I was in a new country, where I did not know anyone or hardly anything. Having always been a deep-feeling, sensitive person, I took on a lot more anger than I deserved. However, because I was such a rookie, I kept my mouth tightly shut. I was determined not to go home this time, to quit as I did with my last job. I could not bear the sense of failure following me again and knew I had to stick it out for as long as possible. Instead, I chose to continue working for a full eight months at the restaurant while I saved up enough money to keep travelling. I finally broke free of these money-making chains once I decided to visit the whole of New Zealand independently. Sure, I was all by myself with just my backpack—and the little bit of money I earned during those long winter months at the restaurant—but I was free.

It was just coming into spring now. Somehow, I sensed the existence of my true love somewhere out there in the world and continuously had mini conversations with him in my head. He was seemingly with me throughout my travels, or perhaps it was the idea of love that stayed present. I inhaled the sweet fragrance of flowers in the air while walking towards my next hostel stop. I knew I would have to stay in well over forty hostels in order to travel the whole country, but I was never sure when I would arrive at each place. I was devoted to allowing synchronicity to guide the flow of my life as often as possible. It had been this way for some time now, and I was beginning to see remarkable results. For instance, I adopted a routine of not knowing where I would sleep from one night to the next. It required courage and awareness to continually trust in the fact that everything would work out in the best-case scenario for me. This kind of faith led me to find like-minded people across my travels. Some even taking me for journeys along with them, which I found especially helpful since I could not drive. They were the kind, open-minded, genuine types that I aspire to be—the sort I was unable to locate in my hometown. Adventuring out into the world caused me to ask more questions and search for answers to the great existential questions in life.

Many nights were filled with the cordial company of these marvellous people I met along the way. Each lovingly shared their own magnificent synchronicity stories filled with the tests and trials they too faced while travelling. Despite any challenges, usually, their stories ended with a deep trust in life. It's as if they also are imbuing their experiences with the glorious palette of synchronicity as she paints the way ahead. As I travelled on a bus to make my way to my next destination, almost having reached the other side of this small country now, I came to a special place. A place I was invited to go to by an older man and his wife who went to this natural park almost every day. As we ascended the mountain, I stopped suddenly and looked over to the clearing on my right. I saw the peak make way to the most fantastic rainbow sunset I've seen yet on my travels. As the seemingly infinite array of natural colour adorned this place with a majesty characteristic of a fantastical kingdom, I suddenly received a vision. This vision was of a time when I stood on this same mountain, but many years before my current lifetime. As I reminisced and imagined what the environment would have looked and felt like during this time, I heard the steady drum of a native tribe nearby. This familiar cadence caused my body to erupt in waves of pleasant goosebumps throughout my being. "Wow...have I been here before?" I whispered to myself.

That same evening, sat near the waters of a glistening mountain lake, I began to write down all of my experiences I'd been having up until now. These visions brought magic to the mundane, even in the dullest of places. But here, these visions come alive in full force! The clean, fresh air and ancient trees spoke to me of my past, present and future all in one chronicle of time and space. I said a prayer to the wind and gave thanks for my life. Having learnt that there is something special about everything was occurring on my journey thus far on my journey. Offering a constant prayer helped me to stay humble to this fact. As I continued writing, more imagery and stories came to me. I began to remember what life was like when we lived in a tribe. My writing free flowed onto the page now.

(Wednesday, November 30th)

When we lived as a tribe, we would all wake at sunrise and do breathwork, movement, and meditation together as a group. After a cold dip in the lake, we would bask in the sunlight to dry off. Depending on the weather, though, some days this was in front of the fire. As we dried, we'd then begin to meditate on the mountaintop to feel renewed, refreshed and awake. We would soak up the warmth and vitality of the flames, flowing intentionally with the song of Spirit, singing and dancing. With such closeness to the brilliance of nature's elementals, we each had our ways of expressing ourselves. We trusted the divine expression in each of us, allowed this to flow and did not doubt our uniqueness. We brought ourselves onto the doorstep of the Great Infinite Universe every morning. Some days were harder than others, but we almost always accomplished a sense of joy and love of life through these sacred rituals.

Briefly, I stopped writing and felt the warm sensations of this vision all over my body as I sat in front of the lake. There was an incredible urge in me to understand if I had just been dreaming, having a vision again, or if this was real. When these 'visions' would happen, it was never clear to me what they were. It was a form of meditation, or maybe imaginative daydreaming, I thought. All of the sounds around me were so real. All of my bodily sensations were so aware and awake during these visions—often more so than in waking life. There was nothing else that made me feel invigorated and in tune with the true nature of life than this. I would move away from life's problems and return to my inner child again, to a truer part of myself. I continued writing once more.

It was the next morning now as I ascended the mountain atop my horse, Whistlefly. The clouds parted ways, and the sunrise erupted before me ablaze with its glistening rays. It's' brilliant orange tones filled up my view, while the previous nights' sky reflected its perfect azure blue tones upon the ocean below. It was a perfect sunrise. No clouds were in sight now to separate the opposing colours. Instead, they blended seamlessly together in a divine spectacle of masculine and feminine energies.

I can feel the brilliant warmth of the sun on my back as though I'm right there. The wind was embracing me, gently reaching through my long dark hair, softly caressing my skin. I was a native woman, and though I looked and felt different, my soul was the same. Suddenly, I became aware of a presence watching me. I couldn't be sure since it was still dark and there appeared to be no one in sight. But my senses tingled atop this mountain letting me know someone was watching me. As if to say 'surprise!' I heard the welcoming call of a nearby eagle and began to laugh, realizing this was the 'watcher' I had sensed. It evoked this sense of liberation in me again, how it felt to be truly free, and how

I always would be. These sacred lands had been gifted to us by mother earth, and it was ours to love and protect just like my heart was.

I remembered how every day I would awaken excited to experience something new. These experiences were often small yet full of joy as nature was always changing. Every day I loved to witness Mother Nature and Father Sky's unique ever-changing patterns and growth. Often this would lead me to find fascinating discoveries of new stone formations or to hear the sweet new sounds of bird songs. With all of these exciting discoveries every day, I felt content with the amount of time I spent alone—I revelled in it. Though, I always worried that I was abnormal to the other tribes' men and women since I enjoyed spending so much time in solitude. These doubts of mine never lasted long; they came and went like a feather in the wind. Deep down in my heart, I knew I was following my life's path—even if I did spend the majority of my time companionless.

As I bathed in the sun's silky, warm rays, I began thinking of all the reasons I was incredibly grateful for this life. My joyous mind then proceeded to think about my future and what I wanted to fill it with—laughter, dancing, art, books, family, friends, and children, I thought. My mood quickly turned as I engrossed myself in what I lacked within the world, reflecting on my long lost kindred soul that I dreamt about almost every day. Though we had not yet met in person, we had met in many of my visions. I loved my independence more than anything but the thought of being able to express abundant love with another gave rise to my inner feminine and maternal instincts. I longed for the day I could teach children of my own about life's many mysteries. I became excited at the thought of it. Watching these little angels grow into beautiful human beings and casting their glorious, unique personalities and talents upon the world would be a wonderful treasure indeed.

My tribe had been travelling all around the realm for as long as I could remember. We had seen so many beautiful landscapes, and I had enough images stored in my mind to paint a whole gallery of breathtaking landscape art. Ellos, on the other hand, was a part of a different tribe. They lived on the same land but further south of this land. Their space was home to very few inhabitants, but some of their tribes' people had previously had quarrels with my tribe. The land of Taureas, where Ellos' tribe lived, had mystifying velvet hues in the night sky by dusk, and turquoise, maroon sky by daylight. Ellos never could decide which he liked better, the feelings he had by the day or the night. Both evoked curious emotions and states of mind for him. He liked to observe his thoughts in the same way an archaeologist might view an unearthed mystery from deep within the Earth: separate in some way, yet intriguing and entirely integrated into the whole.

It was a dazzling summer's morning as he lay by the river, listening to the gentle ambience of the water flowing. As he stared ahead into the distance, his eyes gravitated towards something which it took his breath away. He had not known such purity of feeling could exist within him before. The sunrise cast a remarkable silhouette over what looked like a natural yet mystical feminine form. All he could perceive was a sparkling, shimmering light behind the shape of what seemed to be a woman, atop a horse. He quickly stood up to take a closer look, but she had disappeared behind the rising rays of the sun over the mountain. Neither of them understood the profundity of their connection that day. But this was one of their souls first meeting in a past life.

As Whistlefly and I descended the mountain, I thought about how being a member of the Plaeda tribe was not always sunshine and rainbows. The rules regarding the creation of masterpieces were not taken lightly. My mother and father, renowned members of the tribe, believed every member should push themselves to their absolute creative limit every day. When I wasn't exploring, most of my time was consumed with studying and testing my knowledge and skills related to the many subjects in our tribal curriculum. One of my favourite places of all resided in another dimension in which only my fellow students and I could access during the darkest recesses of the night. As part of this tribal curriculum, we learned the ways of the shamanic dream world and how to navigate consciousness there. The place we went after dark was the great universal cosmic library in which you could read, build, or create anything you could imagine.

Some days were filled with discomfort during this lifetime. We would occasionally battle with nearby tribes and lose members of our family. Though we knew, the family were never too far from us. To us, death was part of the celebration of life. We knew these polarities—light and dark, good and bad—were part of the natural balance in life. Sooner or later, I tried to understand that the light was born out of the darkness every day. The remarkable thing about nature was that it unhooked my mind away from these troubles. The more time I spent in solace with the natural world, the more it charged me. Once charged, I felt inspired by spending time with others in the tribe. Nature made me realise what a gift it was to be a part of a community and live in this world, even though it seemed alarming at times. It satisfied my need of wanting to be alone and made room for my eagerness towards social interaction again. During this time, I realised the innate magic that can occur when two people wish to be in the company of one another.

As I approached the central circle of my tribe after a long day, I heard my father speak of a planet they called "Trapest 1". A star had been discovered in the constellation of Aquarius according to the word of my people. The planets surrounding it were potentially inhabited by life. A new world had been discovered, a sixth-density world named 'Sylvetha', my best friend added. I remembered how my tribe at the time had been making these kinds of discoveries through mass meditation. They had been receiving visions of an orange and pink planet, where time was completely different and where some ancestors came from initially.

As I sat around the campfire, I reached for my bag and unearthed the many different flowers I had picked that day. The flowers were used to make art for the tribe. My elder smiled at me, and I realised I was so lucky that I had been elected for this job, years ago. It was one of my favourite things to do; I was honoured to create art for my tribe. I was always so excited to sit around the fire and listen to everyone's stories of the day. We would talk about the new plant species and animals we had found, sharing about the world from our unique perspectives. The fire would always light up my people's eyes with a phenomenal quality when they talked about their passions. They would sit for hours, laughing, singing, and describing every detail with great feeling and imagination. Their time around the fire made the chief, and all of us, very happy, indeed. As the sun finally set on the evening, I felt blissfully content within my snug little tipi and drifted off into the dream world along with my tribesmen and women.

Suddenly a swift breeze climbed up my back, and my hand stopped writing. It was getting late, and I still had to make it back to the hostel alone. Before going to bed that night—instead of trying to stay asleep in my noisy shared room—I took a walk down the main road in front of my hostel. I looked up, and millions of stars in the sky stared back at me. I could see the Milky Way for the first time in my life with my very own eyes. The beauty of each twinkling star took my breath away. I focused on my breath now, gazing at the stars. Once again, I sensed into the healing capacity of these seemingly far away, yet closeby worlds. I knew that the messages carried in my dreams and visions were of significant importance—only I didn't know how to understand it all yet. I was too concerned with my daily living and still carried unpleasant habits with me like smoking cigarettes and eating junk food.

That same night, I had a dream and felt myself as the embodiment of Divine Feminine energy—active and fierce, yet flowing and receptive. It felt as though I remembered some ancient cosmic royalty. This realisation gently permeated the veil. I saw various lifetimes lived throughout the Great Universal Web of Life. The textures, colours and smells began to come alive all around me. Strange images of animals and environments would swoop in and out of my awareness. It was almost as though I was taking a ride through the vast world of consciousness itself. One thing was certain: I had help during this process—something or someone was guiding me to explore dreams and visions in this way. My angels and ancestors were with me, whispering words of wisdom, during deep inner healing and reflections. I would always come back to the notion that I was never alone.

THE CHRONICLES OF SYNCHRONICITY

THREE

The Sylvethian Realm

∞

During one of my last hostel stays in New Zealand, I am suddenly faced with a full-blown social anxiety attack. I was usually resilient to most energies, but this place was a mess, physically and vibrationally.

I felt overwhelmed by all of the people and energies, which were all crammed into a small room. All of a sudden, my breath began to quicken, and my old fears resurfaced, playing out on a TV screen in my mind. All at once, I began receiving memories from my past struggles. I was feeling overwhelmed and out of control as this panic grabbed ahold of me I needed to try to calm down. Even though I was trying to quit, I gave in to my cravings, stepping outside to have a smoke to calm down.

As I breathed in the familiar taste of tobacco, disappointment came over me for smoking. Not even finishing the cigarette, I flicked it away in shame of what other backpackers would think of me. Instead, I began contemplating recent times spent waitressing at the café. I had worked arduously to apply spiritual principles in order to handle each day. Though the affirmations and karma yoga practises had supported me, I was nevertheless unable to get to the bottom of my social anxiety. It was one of my biggest hurdles to overcome, usually keeping me in a state of unease. This meant I was less able to do my job or any task at all, in fact. I thought back to how much better I could have done as a waitress if it were not for my anxiety.

Rather than musing over hard times, instead, I reminded myself of all the major accomplishments made in my life. As my heart began to settle down with this, I took a long, deep breath. I asked my angels for guidance, and all of a sudden, my memories retook me. I thought back to when I was just coming out of the tail end of my depression. During this time, I had no idea what I would do for money and made some bad decisions to survive that went against my integrity. I chose to go against a quiet voice in my mind that said 'no' at the time, and listened to a louder voice screaming that I needed to do something to pay my rent. This louder voice told me to do whatever it took to pay for my bills at the time, even if it meant working with people I did not trust. This memory often came to me when I was in turmoil, but now, instead of penalising myself for making such mistakes in the past, it served as a testament to always trust in my gut instinct. Here and now though, I was having to face these past decisions I had made in full force as they were coming back to haunt me in different ways.

I decided not to look away from these past mistakes this time. After discussing my faults with a friend, I decided to make a video to my audience who had been following my travelling adventures online. This video discussed my shadows head-on as I was being honest about the mistakes I made in the past. The reason I did this was to stop some internet bullies who were trying to make me feel ashamed of myself for my past mistakes. After many months of scolding myself and fearing the things I had done in the past coming to light in my present, I eventually realised enough was enough. Now, my current hostel surroundings were too much to bear, and I knew I had to start addressing my internal self. This meant firstly forgiving myself and then releasing the words of internet trolls to be given back to where they came from.

I knew that facing my online persecutors—and the feelings that came with doing so—would mean opening up to a very vulnerable state. But I decided it was the only decision I had: to be truthful about my mistakes but be open about the fact that I had moved past this stage in my life now. I now knew this was not the route I was willing to take to survive in the world. All that I had was my heart and soul, and if I were to them to anything less than integral, I would eventually have to face this alone. I learned during my life so far that my soul seemed to check out when I made damaging decisions.

I felt so much fear in coming clean of my past mistakes and putting myself out there honestly. Eventually though, as I received an influx of messages, I burst out into tears. Completely balling on the floor, I read each and every comment. Almost all of which were supportive towards me and honoured me for having been brave enough to tell my story and be honest about my mistakes. I substantiated just how helpful expressing repressed negative memories within our world could be when we have the right people to listen to us. This is where true healing can take place. By having enough courage to express something so personal, I was given reassurance from the listening ears. This provided me with the community I had needed all along to move past these mistakes. It was just one of the tools that Synchronicity had taught me while running a spiritual business online for myself.

Though the company did not pay my rent, it did provide me with a way to connect with other like-minded individuals. Aside from apparently helping others, I also understood that sharing my expression with the world was helping myself to heal at the same time. It was clear how much of a miracle the internet could be when used correctly. It opened so many doors of opportunities for many people I came into contact with.

The next day I returned home to England, not knowing what I would do next and feeling somewhat sombre to be back. I began to lose my connection to Synchronicity and the Sacred Spirit on my return home. Somehow I had lost all of my possessions through transit and had no idea what I would do to pay the bills as I did not want to go out and get another nine-to-five job. I stopped spending so much time in nature. I spent way more time indoors seeking approval on social media to feel better about myself—all of which was a ploy my ego was cleverly using to distract me from doing the healing work that my soul still required at the time.

I was having great difficulty feeling connected to anything or anyone. I especially felt disconnected from myself and spent many lonesome nights crying to sleep. I did not comprehend it at the time, but I was purging a lot of my previous years' experiences still stored in my body. Now that I was back home again, I had the safety and security to readdress these past memories and think about where I was headed in the future. After going on a walk with my family one day, I was unable to connect to nature or the people around me. I decided to lock myself in my room that night, with no distractions, to meditate and seek a vision that would give me answers. Something I had been avoiding doing for several miserable weeks.

As I settled into the familiar state of calmness, I let go of everything I was presently holding on to. My head began to tingle as a new vision began to unveil itself. It came on quickly and with an unexpected vibrancy that shook up my nerves a bit. As I calmed my nerves, I was transported to another timeline in which I stood in front of a closed cave opening. Next to me happened to be someone called Joel, whom I recognised as being part of a mission we were on to find 'something'. Instinctively, within this vision, I began to ground into the Earth while breathing deeply. Standing in front of a closed cave, strangely, my hands started to move in sync with one another. They traced patterns and sacred shapes such as the infinity sign, circles and triangles. My throat chakra also started to buzz, and I could feel some Light Language wanting to flow through me as I spoke the words "Ee-aka lemonushu-te-a, ver-ish-ni ekano-lashuku may-a". As Joel looked at me in disbelief and seemed concerned, roaring noises and rumbling sounds came from within the cave and startled us both. I gasped as I began to see a shimmer of light emanating from inside the cave as the door boulder rolled to the left.

I heard outlandish voices echoing from deep within the stone walls. I could not make out what they were saying, nor could I decipher any particular language. All I knew was that their voices sounded like home. I looked at Joel straight in the face, and he seemed exceptionally uncomfortable as though he was about to run back at any moment. I closed my eyes and decided I was going to do this. My destiny had led me here, and I could hardly stop myself from entering this cave now—even if it meant doing it with my eyes closed.

As we stepped cautiously inside, my eyes caught a glimpse of lush nature climbing up all of the cave walls. There were bountiful breeds of flowers I had never seen before. The caverns were filled with iridescent colours and heavenly aromas. It felt especially magical to be inside this place. There were colourful crystals embedded into the stone walls forming similar sacred shapes to the ones my hands had previously channelled before coming inside. As we approached a golden column, I peeped around the edge of it to see a massive room behind. My heart seemed to beat quicker than the speed of light, as I noticed a fabulous centrepiece carved out of stone with a roaring violet flame fire within the centre of this room.

My eyes hurriedly scanned the whole place from side to side. Once my eyes fully adjusted to the new ecology, I saw women and men all gathered around one another. Their lips were not moving, but I could tell they were somehow engaged in a deep, loving conversation. There were human-like children all playing together, but in a much more developed way than the children I've ever seen. I watched them as closely as I could without bringing attention to myself. From afar, I could see these children were playing some kind of mental-telepathic game which involved moving out of the way of each others' invisible balls of energy. It certainly looked like fun. I then saw a group of beings approaching us. My heart began to beat immediately, and I sensed they could feel it from their short distance away.

These radiant elven-looking beings had a different skin tone and a rainbow-like shimmer to their bodies. They almost looked multi-coloured and had exquisite features. They wore long robes and seemed supernatural and perhaps dreamlike. My eyes caught a glimpse of a particular female approaching us whose 'hair' cascaded down her back, just below her knees—although it didn't look like hair at all. Instead, it seemed like some kind of liquid, watery substance. It was so silky, as though the softness of it would melt if anyone were to touch it. I had never seen a texture or material like this before but assumed it was some kind of plasma. Whatever it was, I knew it was used for high power.

All of a sudden my eyes were overflowing with water, and I tried to control my fast-paced breathing. This was beyond words, it was beyond feeling, and I felt compelled to take it further. Upon sensing this, the woman with water-hair sensed my presence and her hands began to rotate in what appeared to be a ceremonial fashion. As she did so, the rest of her kin stood by her side and turned towards us. I felt my eyes suddenly widen in fear and gasped as I tried to relax into my intention for being there and having found this place. The beautiful female began walking towards me. As she got closer, I froze in disbelief, unable to move. Joel was far behind me at this point, and I could hear him retreating.

I began to hear this woman's voice in my head and realised she was speaking to me telepathically. She asked me in a wise, powerful, yet gentle voice, "What are you doing here?"

"I have come because my intuition and soul lead us here. I gathered all the necessary information on your species' existence, concluded you must be real, and journeyed here to the depths of the Earth feeling that we ought to find you," I replied out loud.

"And what do you want from us?" she asked, intrigued.

To which I replied, "To learn. To know why we are here. To connect."

She turned to look toward Joel and asked, "And this man, who is he?"

"He's a friend. He was able to help locate everything for me," I proclaimed.

She turned to Joel with a look on her face as if to sense into his intent. As she did so, he began to take another nervous step backwards. She looked once more at me and began to walk closer. When she was close enough, she placed a finger on my third eye, and I could feel that she was searching for something within my consciousness.

After a moment, she removed her finger from my forehead, and with a thoughtful countenance said, "I see."

She turned her attention back to Joel. As she began to look into his eyes, he started to cower and become increasingly more uncomfortable. She squinted her huge eyes at him and finally turned her head and said to me, "This man is a liar, I'm afraid. He did not come here for the same reason as you."

Shocked, I looked at Joel and tried to find a shred of remorse or guilt in his face. I automatically knew what she spoke of, but Joel's body language screamed that he was in defensive battle mode and was not about to apologise anytime soon.

With stern resolve, she said, "I'm afraid he will have to leave before we can discuss anything further—unless, of course, he can humble himself and admit his wrongdoings in coming here to take our precious crystals."

I turned my attention to Joel, and with concern pleaded, "Joel, please! You have to admit what you have done wrong and start again with your intention. These beings have no room for insincerity, you are much more than this! Please, admit your mistake and choose to change it right now. They are trying to help us!"

Joel swiftly became angry and started shouting abuse towards these beings, "I have done nothing wrong! I will do no such thing for these aliens! They are ungodly! They will die like the rest of them!! You should have never come here, Ellie!"

I shook my head at Joel. With resolve, I looked deep into his eyes and tried to communicate to him that his last chance was soon to be over. I was receiving telepathic images from the beings that he was going to have to leave this planet for now and be reincarnated back after some studying in the spirit world. Because of his behaviour, his karma would start a new journey so his soul could learn the lessons he regretfully failed in this life.

As if to say, "try me," he glared at us all with an invitation to initiate conflict.

As Joel lunged forward with the intent to strike one of the beings, suddenly, with a subtle flash of light, his body disappeared into thin air! It was as though he had never existed. I looked at the female in shock and averted my gaze towards my feet to stop myself from causing a fuss. Seeing my concern, she calmly explained that they had changed his timeline, for now, so he could learn the lessons of universal love and acceptance. I felt sad knowing that Joel had been getting caught in his socially conditioned fear-body, which could not see beyond the limitations of separateness. Deep down in his Being, I sensed a light within him, but he made his choice as so many have in this world: to forget divinity, and what our soul is really here to accomplish. Clearly, Joel was not ready to proceed further in his journey yet. But all in good time, I thought.

She turned to me and asked, "How did you get past the wall, may I ask?"

Unsure how to answer, I stammered, "The wall...? I... I don't really know... we were stood in front of the cave when all of a sudden the symbols on the boulder looked strangely familiar to me. Then I began to feel fuzzy, like I was remembering a dream, and started channelling shapes and symbols with my hands. The next thing I knew the wall was a pathway, and we walked all the way down here to you. It felt like I was hallucinating this whole time, perhaps I still am?"

Gently, she acknowledged, "You are not hallucinating. You remembered how to come back here from your Higher Self, and it guided you here."

"I remembered? You mean I've been here before?" I asked with intrigue.

"Why, yes of course," she proclaimed.

"When, how, who was I?" I stammered curiously.

As if to be drawing from a prophecy, she announced, "Well, right now you appear to be the lost Alice."

With some amusement in my tone now, "The lost Alice..? You mean like in Alice in wonderland?" I ask. And as if to just realise something peculiar, "but wait, how are you speaking English?" I request.

She smiles, "I am, in fact, speaking my own language but using a telepathic transmitter that translates my language into English for you."

"Oh, I see! Could I hear something in your language?" I ask with curiosity.

Playfully, she replies, "Misco-apethe-a nevo-deam liesath-ape talamista morac e-is moleph."

I was mesmerised. It was so beautiful, and it sounded like a mix between an Elven language with a smooth Celtic twang to it. I smiled as I wondered if this was where my Light Language had its roots.

"Oh, wow! That's amazing!" I admit. Just then, I realised I'd not asked her name, requesting, "What may I call you?"

"Sylvethia," she offers kindly.

Sylvethia led me past her people onto a staircase that seemed to go on forever. She spoke about me being the one who was going to help humanity in a big way and that I would write a book about my time being here with them. After this, she spoke about my mission on Earth and how I ought to find at least three other people to bring back down here with me next time. When I asked why, she told me that the Earth was going to require more Lightworkers in her ascension and that some of us would have to make underground bases to be safe from whatever may occur on the surface of the planet. It seemed as though she was suggesting that only some of the human race would survive whatever would happen in the future. However, just as I thought this, she looked at me and telepathically said, "It does not have to be this way."

Sylvethia began to describe their realms' creation story to me. "In the beginning, there was total love, unity, and wholeness," she said softly. "The universe was complete within itself, a unified field of Being. There was no awareness of itself, it merely was. It encompassed everything, but it was nothing at the same time. Then there was a sudden change: a spark of desire was ignited—the desire was to know itself. This desire propelled the forces of the universe to separate into two contrasting parts. These two parts were known as the masculine and feminine energies. The masculine being that of will and expansion, and the feminine of nurturing and receptivity. And thus life, and duality, was born."

With this, she also mentioned the three primary extraterrestrial races that were involved in seeding human consciousness onto planet Earth. The Lyrians, the Sirians, and the Pleiadians. "The story goes," she continued warmly while motioning her hands back and forth in an elegant fashion conjuring a holographic scene, "that the Founders who reside in a higher dimension had proposed that Earth was ready to inhabit a new species. The Lyrians decided they were going to make a hybrid race of themselves, mixed with the genetics of the race that currently roamed the Earth. As well as this, the genetics of the Sirians and Pleiadians were placed in the mix. The Lyrians wanted to create a race unaware of duality, unaware of good and evil, so to speak. So they created 'Adams and Eves' which roamed the Lyrian curated 'Garden of Eden' for many years. The Sirians, who were involved in the seeding of human consciousness for less integral reasons, had actually begun to warm to the humans and decided that it was against their free will to be unaware of duality."

"They spoke to Adam in the form of a serpent, assuring him that they surely would not die if they were to eat from the Tree of Knowledge (of good and evil)," she shared. "It was that day that humanity decided to understand more about the true reality of their world. In doing so, the Lyrians banished them from the Garden of Eden; and more importantly, from the Tree of Life, their Starchild history, immortality, and Starseed destiny. Then, it was up to the Pleiadians who would have the closest watch over the humans to help them during their navigation through consciousness within this new duality. She went on to speak of our interconnectedness with all things. Each and every one of us on this planet knows each other in some way or another. Before we were born, we decided to create this world for ourselves as gods. We choose to forget each other so that when we would all meet again during Heaven on Earth, we would understand ourselves from a fresh perspective, no longer controlled by our past."

Sylvethia then shared that she is a Queen in her realm.

Introducing me to her other four sisters, Nerika the wood elf, Elya the high elf, Alethia, the fire mage, and Celeste the wind mage. Each sister showed me their own roles within this beautiful realm. Nerika took me on tour around her forest and introduced me to all of her animals. She taught me how to have conversations with each living creature and how they understand everything she asks of them. Then she demonstrated with some squirrels by asking them to find us some food for lunch. They return to us with nuts and berries in their little hands. A beaming smile adorns my face at the overwhelming sensation of adorableness overload. The animals seem to be her little helpers, and they carefully observe me.

Then Elya, the high elf, showed me around her castle, somehow nested within a gigantic waterfall. She taught me how to manifest intentions with the powerful consciousness of water, and how the sacred goddess of water carries all of the memories of the Akash. This Akashic memory stored by the water can be tapped into to retrieve the information of our past and future through love.

The two mages, Alethia and Celeste, came to bid me farewell as I am almost at the end of my tour of the Sylvethian Realm. Alethia shows me how she conjures the element of fire through her hands to heal people and transmute their pain and suffering, transforming it into strength and passion. Celeste it seemed, worked very closely with her sister, Queen Sylvethia, with her skills of high intelligence and wisdom. Celeste is incredibly useful in giving the Queen advice and knowledge. She carried the sword of intellect, which she uses to keep the realm protected and safe. Sylvethia does not speak to me of her powers, but I sense that she is a Goddess of the ethereal realms, and uses this to be a great Queen to her people. As I hug them all goodbye, I say a silent prayer to myself that I wish to be back again. Sylvethia smiles at me and speaks to me in Light Language. Before I have the chance to reply, I am brought back to my little room in England by the sound of my mother knocking on my door.

THE CHRONICLES OF SYNCHRONICITY

FOUR

Evia And Elias Find One Another

∞

WHILE KATE WAS finishing her tour of the Sylvethia Realm, Ethan had a profound experience after a wedding ritual he attended. He came face to face with a powerful storm, awakening a Kundalini experience within him.

Leading up to this wedding, Ethan consistently prayed every day as he was feeling called to experience more of the truth about life. On the day of his Aunt's wedding rite, Ethan spotted several archetypes; specifically, one from the Arthurian Legend "Sword in the Stone," and another, a Druidic ceremony taking place around a sacred cauldron. Even though everyone had their shoes on, Ethan took his shoes off and stood with his bare feet directly on the grass. Using his breath and inner vision, he fully breathed into his surroundings and connection to Spirit. He could feel every aspect of the rite being performed and began receiving mental downloads of the deeper meanings behind what was happening all around him.

Following this, everyone attending the wedding participated in a Pagan ritual all together as a family. At this time, Ethan heard a voice in his head beckoning him to allow energy to flow through his hands for the sacred rites being facilitated that day. While doing so, the voice spoke again and informed him about the true meaning of this wedding rite. It was much more than just a wedding, it was a cosmic solar body integration ceremony, meant for initiates of great truth and love.

As Ethan took part in this marriage ritual entirely, and began to feel an energy buzzing in his feet. It travelled from the Earth, heavenward through his spine. Once the ceremony was complete, he felt lighter energetically and went to dinner with all the family. Noticing a sacred feminine statue on the way, he performed a prayer, placing one of the red crystals he had brought with him—without knowing why—under the root chakra of the statue.

During supper, Ethan was guided by a new voice in his head. It communicated to approach everyone with absolute loving kindness from the heart, and clarity from the mind. Before leaving to drive home, Ethan mentioned to the high priest that his God-self was now fully activated and thanked him for his time. The priest replied and said, "It's about time!" Then as Ethan approached his car, the priestess ran to him and prophesied that he was about to go through his very own "high-way" driving test. She mentioned in passing that the energy of this ritual was a first for them also, it had been profoundly powerful. Ethan immediately intuited what the women had meant. He was going to receive a consciousness test in some form or another, one from his higher-self to engage his spiritual evolution.

On the drive home, Ethan is met with a wild storm that had become very turbulent. Instead of turning back, he had the instinct to follow the GPS directly, even though it was taking him on a longer route than planned. As Ethan steered his car down a back road, he was suddenly faced with an intense storm. There was thunderous booming, blinding lightning strikes struck all around. He was now in the heart of this massive rain storm. Powering his way through, he came to a place on the road where a tree had blown down, blocking his passage. Ethan had no way to cross and peculiarly decided to dress down and go outside to greet the storm. Then he realised how good the rain felt again his skin and knew why. Ethan greeted the thunder and lightning head-on. He chose to honour Zeus and Hera with a crystal gifted to each, placed into some water under a tree. After finishing a quick energy routine in the rain, Ethan got back into the car intending to back up where he had come from.

He got dressed and was just about to back up as he saw a set of headlights approaching. Inside the truck, he saw a man and woman smiling at him. The man rolled down his window, and with a glow in his eyes he asked, "Do you need a hand? We know to carry the right tools in this neck of the woods." He laughed and proceeded to carry a chainsaw from the back of his truck and cut up the fallen tree. The path was suddenly clear.

The whole experience led Ethan into what would be a two-week psychic activation, a huge heart opening, and a sense that he was reborn spiritually in the world. After many exhilarating and unexplainable experiences, the two weeks were finally over. Ethan was then told that he was still too weak to maintain the energy flow required for this level of activation. He understood that the elements had facilitated this experience, and would do so again. Eventually, it would be an ascension activation that was more in alignment with a grander vision, that even he could not yet see.

Ethan sat in his bountiful garden space the morning after and began pondering the experiences he had during those two weeks. He felt a new lease of life in having gone through something so indescribably magnificent. The experience had been a state of heightened awareness and joy—which enabled him to co-create in ways he had never been taught before. He had experienced some kind of 'superpowers' after this wedding rite. A realisation dawned upon him that human beings had only just scratched the surface of their capabilities. We were with many more 'helpers' than we could ever imagine.

...

After my mind-blowing vision of The Sylvethian realm, I felt more grateful for every passing day, more than ever before. I started going out into nature again meditating, practising Light Language, and singing to the trees. A few weeks later, my brother and I drove to a nearby restaurant. On the drive, I noticed a sign with an Om symbol next to it and made a mental note to find out what this place was about. The next day I awoke in the early morning, determined to go and visit this building as it was only a twenty-five-minute walk from our home.

Inside, I approached the front desk to be greeted by the smell of incense and a woman by the door. I asked what kind of services they provided, she spoke of their spiritual meditations and healings. Just then I noticed yet another Synchronicity to surprise me again. She told me that this was an ashram in which a Guru came to facilitate healing and guidance for the local people. I was gobsmacked at this amazing coincidence as this was precisely what I had been looking for. The universe manifested this place so close to home for me. Previous to my travelling this ashram did not exist. This newfound community gathering created a warmth within my heart. It's location was especially surprising since my hometown had not appeared open-minded to such practises. I felt excited to finally connect with like-minded individuals and took regular classes there.

Spending several months visiting this place I realised that the vibe no longer resonated with me. However, the day that I had a Darshan session with the woman at the head of the organization changed something within me. Darshan involved staring into an enlightened persons eyes, and imaginal healing would take place.

After this session, she had asked me, "What are you struggling with?" I told her I could not seem to find my soul mate. She smiled and consoled me. That same night, I had a vision while my eyes were open. It felt like I had dreamt about this place before, like Dejavu dreaming or something. Though, it was some kind of astral travel and not a dream. I looked around at my surroundings and saw I had been transported to a beach. I felt perfectly happy to bask in my own company there, along with its natural beauty.

The elements here felt purer than anywhere else. Seemingly untouched, the sea was a cerulean, transparent blue. The sky an azure, violet-pink sunrise which was all I had ever dreamed of. I noticed that no negative thoughts came to me whatsoever while I inhabited this place. It was a space of peace only. The air was filled with the sweetest smell of fresh flowers mixed with sea salt, and I noted only the sound of birds and crashing waves all around me. The sea was calm, and the lulling waves began to send me into a blissful trance. As I buried my bare feet in the crystal-like sand, I spotted the sun glistening on top of the turquoise water. It's serene beauty beckoning me to come and take a dip in its refreshing waters. I answered the call, entering the seas, and my whole body felt embraced by the warmth of the gentle lapping waves. As I began to swim, the water caressed every area of my body. My lungs felt lighter than ever as I breathed in this tranquil feeling.

I knew this place was far from my home planet, everything was so pure, nature fully flourished! As I floated atop the water, my imagination briefly flashed to the thought of him. This mystery man whose name I did not know. Though somehow I had always known it began with the letter E. I didn't quite know what he looked like, I only remembered how it felt to be with him. As I smiled to myself, I heard a whisper tickle my eardrums. I calmly opened my eyes and looked to where the sound appeared to be coming from.

Although I felt startled at the presence of him an exhilarating feeling of love encapsulated me now. All I could see were his chocolate brown eyes, they rested in a smouldering state of joyfulness. I heard his voice inside my head whisper, "Hello beautiful." With a shy but coy smile, I replied, "How are you?"

"Tranquil," he retorts.

Slowly I replied, "your name is E…"

"Elias, yes."

With leaps of enthusiasm coming over me now, "I must show you this place," I squealed as we swam together back to the shore.

"You must," he laughed warmly.

"Anything you can think of, all we've ever dreamed of, it's all here in this place!" I reveal.

"Ahh yes, show me… I've waited long enough," Elias said in quiet relief.

Standing on the golden sand now, I thought of having a collection of crystals. Suddenly the urge to speak in light language overcame me while I motioned my hands back and forth. Underneath the wet sand, I unearthed some amethyst, rose quartz and opalescence crystals. I smiled mightily and played with the energy surrounding us, and directed it to encompass our energy fields.

From there on out, I let myself be a vehicle for my soul's expression. I began to hear music and started to sing and dance in a complete trance of blissful self-expression. Elias watched me like no one ever had. Our connection was older than time, more than words. We were in our purest forms of masculine and feminine during these moments. Polar opposites, yet drawn together with a natural attraction, like magnets. I began to dance around him in my colourful garments, and reached for his hand. He readily accepted mine and we danced the day away, our hearts continuing to grow closer, beating as one. Instinctively, Elias touched chakra points along my spine which sent me into a state of euphoria as he energized each energy centre..

Elias immensely enjoyed watching his beauty-to-be unfold like a rose flower, each petal unfolding softly. Evia lit up with a light from within as she felt the energy between them bursting at the seams. I truly felt like a goddess, honoured in all of my glory. All of a sudden, I had an idea, and as I looked at him, I shrieked ecstatically, "Let's paint a picture of this day so we can remember it forever!"

There were no limitations here in this magical space; everything you wanted to wish for you could do or be. They decided to play a game in which neither were allowed to see the others painting until it was finished. Miraculously, they stood in front of their newly born art canvasses and began to artistically express themselves. They used freshly picked flower paints to colour with. Together, they laughed and shared stories together about all of their recent experiences. Many of which would usually be undertaken with fear or doubt, they realised, but in this place, they were so free.

Once complete, they revealed their creations and were overjoyed to see they had painted one another. A divine masculine image in all of its brilliance, together with the sun and fiery elements made up her portrait of him. He, of course, painted the divine feminine, cool tones, majestic hues of blues and purples, which made up his starry sky and moon portrait. She embodied all that was natural and had the most beautiful circular symbols and shapes surrounding her silvery figure. This entranced Evia, she could not imagine feeling more drawn to him at that moment.

As the day began losing light and the first signs of the stars were upon them, Elias asked Evia to sit down in the sand while he performed some energy work on her. She knew it was going to send her into a state of euphoria just by the mere closeness of his presence. Tingles began spreading all up and down her spine as he lay down beside her. He placed his hands just above her heart, barely touching her chest. She felt the effects were opening her heart chakra.

These effects seemed to be reaching beyond her astral body to the other side, where her body resided. Elias was healing the wounds that her physical body carried on the Earthly plane. After a few minutes, only love remained in her heart for him and for all living things. As he leant in closer, they began to share one another's breath. It almost seemed like she could see this magical energy entering her body, it was pure and made her soul shiver with pleasure.

Suddenly, she witnessed a rainbow coloured energy emanating all around them. It was love, and she could see it. Evia felt more alive now than ever before. It seemed they were creating increasing amounts of energy by the second, and neither of them could wait any longer for their bodies to touch. Finally, they kissed and slowly began to make what felt like everlasting love.

This time making love was different. Euphoric, energetic love was pouring into them, balancing their whole being. Energy rising slowly as they breathed through the whole body, and finally exploding in the crown chakra. At this moment, they felt themselves immersed in a oneness sphere. Every motion, was in sync with the other, and all things. It felt as though it was an eternity before they laid to rest together and Evia whispered sincerely, "So this is what heaven feels like?"

"No doubt about that," he replied.

Suddenly bliss turned to worry upon realising their time together had almost come to an end. They were going to wake up soon.

"Why can't we stay here forever?" I asked him.

"Because, it doesn't work," he paused, "...until we can find one another on the earthly plane".

I arose to look at him. "What if we never find each other on the physical plane?" I asked melancholically.

"We will. When we do find each other, neither of us will be sure. We will be filled with worldly doubt, fear, and the conditioning of our past life experiences. Therefore, we have to become intuitive enough to decipher when we have found each other. There are many distractions and other temptations out there—we both must be strong."

"Why can't we just ask one another on the earthly plane if we remember this night?!" I asked.

"We cannot, Evia. Our souls must first dream one another up, and then find one another through Synchronicity. It's a puzzle playing game. Otherwise, these memories may fade, even more so than they will when we go back to Beta brain shortly," Elias proclaimed.

"Wait a minute!" his eyes lit up with light.

Before Evia, he presented a purple and green ring, with four diamonds for the four corners. She smiled, laughed and placed her hand on her cheek in gleeful joy.

Holding out the ring, Elias shared, "This is a crystal that belonged to you many millions of years ago. It was lost when the great disaster happened, and we were separated. But when I found it eight years ago I remembered everything from my past lives, I remembered you. I wished and longed for the day that I would see you, that you would visit me someway somehow, and tonight you did."

"When I think I've found you, without us voicing anything of this night to one another, I will present you with this ring."

"But how does that help you to know?" I asked, confused.

He looked unsure.

"I will present you with a ring the same night that we meet," He affirmed confidently once more.

I nodded in agreement.

Suddenly, my phone began to buzz. "Time for tea," a text message read. I stopped writing and carried the buzz of this romantic vision with me into the rest of the evening. At the time, I did not realise how profound this vision would later be. This vision was a key catalyst to help unfold my path to love. I came to understand the feeling body paired with non-attachment to a glorious dream, could bring about the heart's desires. Even though it was experienced through the imagination, the power of the feeling attached to this vision would be enough to bring this manifestation into the physical plane.

EVIA AND ELIAS FIND ONE ANOTHER

THE CHRONICLES OF SYNCHRONICITY

FIVE

Kate and Ethan Synchronistically Meet

∞

One misty morning, as I gazed out of my office room window, I was scrolling through some messages and noticed a name that stood out to me. A man named Ethan had sent me a message about my previous 'Light Language in Nature' video. He mentioned how this video had made him feel deeply connected to a shared truth between us. He detailed how he, too, had a deep sense of reverence and love for nature. It seemed we shared a similar passion and love for spirituality and for Mother Nature. I was overwhelmed with excitement to read Ethan's messages. He was an excellent wordsmith. His words spoke to my soul in an ineffable manner. I began to wonder who this mystery man was and thought about him all afternoon. We hit it off and began regular correspondence on all things nature and spirituality.

A few weeks later, and after many Skype calls with Ethan, I began feeling that this was all too good to be true. Instead of worrying about a romance, we decided we would be more like friends or close allies.

It was nearing my twenty-third birthday, and I decided to go and stay at my Dad's apartment in Spain. My conversations with Ethan continued to become more exciting every day. Not a moment passed wherein we were not sharing something together. As I sunbathed next to a pool area, in the glorious heat of the Spanish sun, I found myself enjoying listening to a Spanish family nearby. Even though I had no idea what they were saying—since I did not understand the language—the way they interacted together made me feel warm and homely inside. Somehow, it made me think of how the resonant tones of a word are perceivable to the heart. This made me realise how Light Language worked. It was a type of 'channelling' that came through me every now and again. It always carried loving intention and gratitude. I began to feel a great sense of peace wash over me as I watched how this family interacted with one another. They seemed to really understand and fully facilitate the sacred qualities of a family. I felt a deep pang of loneliness overtake me, and as I thought to message Ethan, I saw his name vibrating on my phone.

"Hello" I answered, elongating the 'o' to reassure him that I was happy to see his call.

"Well, hello beautiful, what are you up to?" he responded.

I proceeded to tell him about this wonderful Spanish family and how amazing it was to see such camaraderie. All of a sudden, I began to hear Ethan's voice lower as though he was about to tell me something difficult.

"I have to tell you something. You remember the crystal reading I did for us about our relationship to one another? Well, I got it all wrong. Instead of being a friend and a close ally in my world, it turns out the crystal that represents you is directly opposite me, with the rose quartz of unconditional love between us." He was referring to a stone casting he performed to understand more deeply what our relationship was going to be all about. Ethan felt so magnetically attracted to Kate that he wanted to make sure he didn't make a mistake in proclaiming his feelings without first being assured it was the right move.

Knowing precisely what he was trying to say, I felt the urge to question him and why he had got the first reading wrong. After much deliberation, I told Ethan I was unsure whether we were meant to be together and to just stay friends, for now. It seemed less complicated, after all, since we lived across the world from one another. After Ethan tried to describe all the reasons we should be together, we ended the confusing conversation. Still, I could not help but carry a huge smile on my face all day.

After a few hours of going through what Ethan had said in my own mind, I thought about the possibility of going to meet him in Canada. I allowed myself to fantasise about what it would be like to be romantically involved together. Later that night, while sat on the balcony of my Dad's apartment, I called Ethan on Skype. Somehow, I felt myself falling in love with every word, every minute of our conversation. The idea of us being together was finally clicking in even though I was not willing to admit it at the time—mainly due to my inherent stubbornness.

It did not take long for Ethan to accept the idea of me coming to visit him. I was the one who did all of the travelling after all and was headed back to England the following day. The night before my plane ride to Canada, I took a long walk in nature and could feel that this was the last time I would walk these hills as the Kate I knew now. Somehow, I knew that this visit with Ethan was going to change everything. I knew I was going to be a completely different person after my visit to see him. I cried some tears out on my walk for the inevitable shedding our my old self. All of a sudden the wind picked up, and I felt the warm embrace of a brand new cocoon surrounding my being. A new adventure awaited me, and I was ready.

...

After finishing the soggy, sugary plane food, I decided to try and get some sleep for the remaining few hours of my flight. I was used to long haul flights by now, but this one seemed to be taking forever. Another hour had passed, and I gave up trying to quieten my mind. Instead, I listened to some chillstep music. So many thoughts were stirring inside and I was simply too full of exhilaration and anticipation to fall asleep. As I thought of Ethan and our soon-to-be meeting, I was met with a feeling that turned into a vision.

My inner world felt a warm, homey feeling, which unfolded into an environment—typical of my now common visionary explorations. I saw myself in a circular clearing of trees within a gigantic forest. The clearing faced a lush cliff filled with vines and flowers, thick with greenery. At the centre of this cliff was a massive, majestic waterfall. The water tumbled and swirled off of the many smoothe-looking rocks collected at the bottom of its surface. As I fully entered this place, smelling the fresh air, I began to have the warmest feelings of home yet—a deep remembering feeling, blissful and calm. I wondered if this was the exact feeling of passing through the light on the other side of the veil.

I see myself wearing robes and a fitted colourful cloak of some kind. Next to me is a man wearing similar regalia and his presence reminds me of that of a king. As some people—about thirty men and women—begin to gather around us within this clearing, I feel a sense of motherly affection towards them. I recognise the feeling and assume that these people are very near and dear to my heart. They seem like a 'light-soul-tribe' family to me. I can see myself in this forest clearing now motioning everyone to be quiet as I am about to tell them some important news. As I do, the man beside me turns to me and whispers, "are you really going to do this?" I look at him with an ache in my heart and reply, "I have no other choice."

Turning to face these people I feel immense respect and care for, I proclaim, "Dear ones; you have all made me so proud. Your sacred ways of teaching many souls who have come and gone will live on forever within the records of the Akash. I am so proud, humbled, and honoured to have spent this sacred time with each and every one of you. It is with great sadness I announce the ancient prophecy we are all familiar with is finally upon us. We must take a stand as the wars on the other side of this universe can no longer be ignored if we are all to live our truth." I finished these words with a firm countenance to make up for the fear I see in each and every one of my people's faces. A great uproar of chaos erupts amongst the people, and they begin to talk frantically, shaking their heads in disbelief.

I begin to see the vision shift now as I am stood before a door that I have never seen before. As I entered, I am brought back to the forest by the sound of my King's voice ordering, "Silence, please! My lady has returned from a meeting with the great council of old, The Founders, and you will listen closely."

I began explaining to these dear people in great detail all about my experience in entering the Realm of Beginnings. A place so few had ever been granted access to. After meeting with our oracle and performing a sacred ritual practise, deep within the forest, I enter a portal through time and space. At the other end of the entrance, a bright room greets me. I walk down what appears to be a glass hallway with mirrors covering almost every inch of the walls. I describe to my people in detail how my instincts told me that the mirrors were a preparatory procedure used before entering the sacred space of The Founders. To access, one must genuinely reflect upon one's soul with the utmost truth and authenticity.

I turned the corner at the end of this hallway, to see a large door before me. The door handles were square-shaped diamonds, filled with abstract lines and colours of pink, purple, blue and green. The door patterns reminded me of some kind of modern Art Deco style. As I touched the door handle, I feel a great sense of trepidation; yet, I can sense the divine timing of this meeting. I remember that my ancestors are with me and have been waiting for this day for a long time.

Upon entering the room, I quickly note the presence of eight beings, all of which were from different lineages and genetics. All of these beings—except two, a male and a female—I sense are from the same galactic family grouping as my people. As I take a seat at the edge of the table, everyone stands up to welcome me in their own languages. I nod, smile, and put my hands together in a prayer position to honour their greetings. The two beings look to be of an unidentifiable lineage to me. I sense the presence of Lyrians, Sirians, Pleiadians, Orions, Arcturians, and Zeta Reticuli, but these beings I am entirely unsure of. I make a mental note to find out their origins before leaving this place.

Just as I am about to speak, a mantis looking creature nods at me and asks, "Prescia, what news do you speak of from the Lands of Intuition?"

I spoke to my people within the forest now, just as I had spoken to The Founders that day. With sincerity and clarity, I proclaim to them, "The Great Oracle of the Enchanted Elm tree has spoken of the calls for aid by planet Gaia. She has beckoned for us across the universe."

I tell them of my Elders' prophecies and how there would come a day that those of us on this side of the galaxy would eventually have to answer Gaia's call. This call for aid would affect the future of every one of us. I tell them that the time has come for those of us who are ready. Those who integrated negative and positive polarities into balance, and graduated from the wisdom school of ancient mysticism—with which our forefathers built this very universe—are called forth. Now is the time to answer the call and usher forward a new age of peace. We are to unite on this mission of spreading the word far and wide. Gaia requires many of us to help her and humanity. During this period of great awakening, we are to help others on this planet—all so that we may progress on our own evolutionary phase. After hours of deliberation, these beings of light send me away to bring forth the mission.

I look lovingly into the faces of my people and continue, "It is here, dear ones, that my time has come to an end. A new adventure must begin." As I see the weary looks in my people's eyes, I turn to my King, and he exclaims "I am with you!" I hugged him tightly, knowing it would be the last time in these bodies. I then turned to my tribe, explaining to them that I will need some assistance in this mission on Earth and in recalling where our souls genuinely call home. I knew that what I was suggesting to my people seemed akin to an ultimate death sentence. All of them had already been through many great wars of consciousness from Orion to Mars and Earth. The thought of reincarnating back onto Gaia at this time, with so much polarity, seemed hopeless. I reminded them of the prophecies of our ancestors and how we knew this day would finally come. We knew that one day, some of us would have to leave our heavenly sanctuaries and go back to where it all started. If we were ever going to heal the rift that was created, and progress further as a species.

"We have one reason to succeed in this mission: the gift of Gaia. She is awakening at a more rapid pace than any of our Elders had prophesied. When we go back there, we will not be met with the same intolerance of spirituality and oneness. Instead, we will find many other soul groups incarnating at the same time from fellow star systems. We will all be there totake care of Gaia and straighten out the last remnants of that which we dare not look: our disowned shadow selves."

"To live as a human once more will be a great adventure; indeed. They are, after all, the pioneers of our future. We will gain so much more knowledge, wisdom, unconditional love, and understanding of our place within the universe once we complete this mission. Our souls will advance from this experience, and even The Founders agreed with this notion. We, too, still face the toils of war, even here amongst the Lands of Intuition. We cannot go forward until we go back to heal what has been broken."

The crowd continued to listen with bated breath, still in complete shock and silence.

"It will not be easy, and everything we have learned during our many years here will be forgotten for a time. We must trust in our souls and spirit guides to retrieve our truth. They will help us to remember our heritage so that we may carry great wisdom and peace into our futures. Those of you who feel called to join my King and me on this endeavour will be part of the Violet Soul Group, facilitated by The Founders. We will meet again during our time on Earth, and come back to our sense of familiar community once more. Those of you who decide to stay here will be the protectors of our lands, and we ask that you hold space and resonance. Practise meditation every day to guide us along our way."

The crowd nodded, and once I beckoned those forward who felt called to accompany us during this mission, two people stepped forth to join us. Both of them felt a deep call from within that they should also be the ones to reincarnate back onto the Earth. They too felt a karmic pull to put an end to unfinished business. I looked around at this magical forest, knowing that this would be the last time I would lay eyes on it as Queen. It felt like madness to ever leave such a beautiful place, but I knew it was for the highest good of all.

Suddenly, I heard a voice from the aeroplane telecom, which loudly proclaimed, "We will shortly be landing in Canada, make sure all electrical items are safely stored away for landing." I was flabbergasted and entranced by what I had envisioned. I could hardly wait to get off the plane to meet what I hoped would be the man of my dreams and tell him all about it. I wondered if he would think I was completely crazy or not for giving any value to such visions. Still, I knew I had to tell him.

As I walked out onto the parking space for arrivals, I saw Ethan's smiling face behind a bouquet of flowers. We awkwardly, yet lovingly, momentarily embraced for the first time. Then, as we drove off, I felt oddly calm to be driving alongside him. It felt so good to see him in person instead of through a computer screen. Ethan pulled over and asked if I wanted to ground in nature after the long trip. I readily agreed since long haul flights generally left me feeling spacey. Sat on some riverbanks in between motorways, with my bare feet on the Earth, I relayed my vision to Ethan and watched his facial expressions closely. He was in total amazement of this vision, and he too began to wonder if he was the King within my imagination, as he said it all sounded so familiar. I smiled and began to wonder what meeting his family would be like.

Later that night, more synchronicities played out between us as we got into riveting conversations together about our connection. It turned out that I had initially named my website after his last name, several years before us even being aware of the existence of each other. I also told him about my different visions and how there was also the fact that I would meet my soulmate there. Every time this soul mate had a name beginning with the letter E. Then suddenly Ethan pulled out a small box from his pocket. I could not believe what I was seeing and thought it must just be an expensive gift. A voice in my head told me it was much more, it was indeed an engagement ring. Ethan handed me the box, and upon opening it, I saw two rings, one purple, and one green. At first, I could not get over the fact that this man had proposed to me the very same day he had met me. It was too much for my ego-mind not to assume that he was somehow crazy and was secretly going to turn out to be a maniac.

My deepest fears surfaced, and I told Ethan I could not accept his ring. Instead, he offered it to me as a promise ring, a promise of love, to which I could not decline.

We had planned to spend our time together at a lake house. As we arrived, we found ourselves in a mini paradise, and we had it for the week! On the way back to England after the most magical time of my life. I remembered how 'Elias' from my vision had presented 'Evia' with a ring. How he had told her of his plan to do so. I could not believe the synchronicity, it was the most potent experience of providence that I had ever experienced. I had a fantastic time putting all of the pieces of the puzzle together on my way home. I realised the many 'coincidences' that had already occurred between us could not be ignored. Whether the ring, the names, and the pure magnetic attraction to one another were all coincidence or not—I began to really trust in the universe and felt an immense amount of love begin to rise up inside of my body.

Once I arrived home in England, I felt elated and extra energy pulsed through me daily. Though, I spent only a few short months in England before I ran back to Canada again. I could not wait to spend more time with Ethan as I missed him so much. This was the beginning of our new life together. I enjoyed living in Canada, but I was greeted once again by my social angst as it came time to meet Ethan's family and friends. Within just the first few months of meeting Ethan, I had released many deep fears and insecurities that I carried with me for a long time. For instance, I would usually feel the need to cover up my face with makeup as I would consistently blush during social interactions. But on the night of New Year's Eve, I decided to go to Ethan's friend's party with no makeup on. All because Ethan had sincerely assured me that did not need it.

I began to feel genuinely liberated to be myself, no longer looking for someone to accept me. Nor did I feel the need to hide from anyone or anything anymore. Ethan's love had begun to heal me in more ways than I could have ever imagined, and it was just the beginning.

THE CHRONICLES OF SYNCHRONICITY

SIX

The Ayahuasca Journey

∞

FAST-FORWARD TO a whole new year later. The synchronicities continue to multiply for us both in mini and macro ways. The relationship between Ethan and I continues to thrive in love. We were moving ever-quickened toward a deeper understanding of ourselves in the world.

Even so, as we were still largely unsure of the path moving forward, our wallets and purses continued to get lighter and lighter. This was largely from fluctuations in jobs. After reviewing the possible reasons for this, we noticed that our lower chakras needed more energy. In reflection, we realised that they had been kicked out from under us at a young age—though for a greater purpose. Being an empath, it rarely felt secure out in the social world. This was apparent when it came to the way I dealt with money, too—a common collective experience for many Empaths across the world. When we do not feel stable and secure within, our root chakra becomes out of balance and seemingly struggles to flow energy through to reach a deservedness of abundance. We did not let this deter us though and continued to try and figure out how to make ends meet, while still living a joyful, free life.

One evening, Ethan found he was let go from his job again. However, with a stroke of luck, he landed a position with a spiritual website the very next day. Not only did he land himself another job working from home, but we were both given the opportunity to visit an Ayahuasca retreat in Costa Rica. It happened to fall on my birthday, and all we had to do was pay for our flights. It felt like a fantastic gift from the universe. This was an incredible surprise for us, and synchronicity came to save the day again as we had been struggling to know which way to turn next. Now we knew we were about to take a different journey, one that involved getting back in touch with Mother Earth.

Several years back, I had watched a documentary, based in the Amazon jungles. It detailed the accounts of people and their experiences with Ayahuasca—a sacred entheogenic plant brew touted for its profound healing abilities. I was fascinated by the idea that a plant could provide medicine for the soul. Ayahuasca was, after all, a sacred plant medicine revered and honoured by many for its healing capabilities. At the time, after watching this documentary, I remember saying to myself, "I will try this someday." It was a whole three years later until I would be ready to welcome the idea of going through with a ceremony, however. Being invited to come to this luxury retreat to understand and experience this plant medicine for ourselves was something we felt eternally grateful for. We knew it was going to change our lives forever.

The day before our trip to Costa Rica, I was frantically worried about my own job situation. I could no longer dedicate my days to creating content for my spiritual website. It was simply not earning enough money to pay the bills. The night before the trip, I scanned a job-listing page. On the first page, I saw the title 'Online English Teacher.' I was instantly drawn to apply and sign up for an interview since I had previously graduated from university with a degree in teaching English. Although I knew that teaching English was not my true passion, it was my back up plan. I was willing to try anything to progress forward in life. The idea of being an online teacher from home seemed like a massive break from the stress and turmoil I had been experiencing in past jobs. I was due to start working a few days after returning home from Costa Rica.

Once we had arrived and had settled in, we began to soak up the energies of this luxurious retreat. The air seemed to be filled with light energy, as though there was higher resonance surrounding this place. The main area had a beautiful pool and dining space, which provided an all-day buffet of whole foods. The rooms were spacious and clean, and there was a touch of luxury added to the yoga and meditation areas as they were surrounded by garden greenery. We went to several classes the following two days there, which were filled with a lot of wisdom from fantastic teachers and speakers. We both resonated with the teachers and people at this place. Everyone had come from all around the world, each with different stories. We were taught how to understand the psychology of the mind, how to use breath-work to calm negative emotions. Finally, we were prepared for our Ayahuasca ceremony through various cleansing herbs and check-ups. The whole place felt safe and sacred, I could not wait for the first ceremony to finally begin.

The doors to the first ceremony opened around seven pm, and we were the first to choose our mattresses for the night. We gathered as a group of about sixty souls around the shamans who would be on hand to help us during our journey. We were guided to use the intention: "merge me back with my soul at all costs". The shamans explained to us that many of our souls were potentially fragmented and had become disassociated from our bodies when we were still very young. Therefore, it was up to us to merge back with our inner child—to look back into our deeply repressed memories and shadows and take responsibility to retrieve our souls again.

I felt ready to greet Ayahuasca, despite some horror stories I had witnessed online and heard others experiencing during their journeys. We were all well prepared to hear and see all kinds of purging happening from ourselves and others. We were informed not to trust a fart and that some means of purging could be sharts, crying, and vomiting, or other things like yawning and sweating.

Before the music started,, we took turns receiving some rapé—a powdered sacred tobacco-based substance—which was blown up our nostrils through a wooden straw. Ethan and I found this to be the most uncomfortable part of the ceremony. It burned, and it intensely inhabited the senses for a moment. Shortly thereafter, there was a sense of grounding.

This was a tool, the shamans said, that was used to clear out the sinuses and prepare the initiate for their travels with the plant medicine. As I approached the shaman for my first cup of Ayahuasca, I looked directly into her eyes to express my readiness for this experience. As she handed the cup to me, the shaman did a prayer on the brew. As is the custom, I simultaneously spoke to Ayahuasca, asking her to help merge me back with my soul before I took a sip. The taste was not particularly terrible, nor lovely. It tasted a bit like soil with some kind of spice. I swallowed the mixture and felt somewhat dizzy from the excitement of it all. Some felt terrified, others excited and hopeful, and I could sense it all at the same time. I walked back to my mattress and laid down silently. We had thankfully chosen the room closest to the nature garden. I aimed to connect with Mother Nature, as she had always provided comfort in my most difficult moments in life. We each had our own mattress and several inches of space in between them. During the ceremony, we were not permitted to speak with anyone but the shamans, instead we were to go inward, to experience Ayahuasca entirely.

Forty minutes into having drunk the brew, I began to feel sensations and tingling starting to happen all throughout my body. Since it was late at night, I could already see colours and shapes forming in the dark. Ethan was nearby on his mattress. I could not help but look over every once in a while to check if he was okay. I began to feel Mother Aya overtake my whole body. First, it started with a vision in my third eye. The vision was of a fractal psychedelic train coming towards me, very slowly, with lights that were gradually getting brighter. I heard a voice tell me that by the time the train had fully arrived, I would be encompassed in a full-blown journey with the medicine. The visuals then took me into a deeper connection with this otherworld within. I breathed and repeated my intentions of loves expansion and understanding.

After the first few bouts of uncomfortably in my body, I felt relaxed and grounded somehow throughout this experience. I was continually able to sense into the group energy, which was both uplifting and scary at the same time. Grounding and elevating all at once felt like swimming as a fish, up and down, side to side, as my energy focus balanced internally. It seemed I could sense into my body more readily as I was journeying throughout different thoughts and emotions. There was an awareness of something much bigger than me playing out, which was indescribable.

There, too, were moments of panic as I experienced the medicine more fully. As I felt uncomfortable in my body one minute, I could hear sounds from others nearby who seemed nervous as well—some even groaning and voicing this discomfort. My inner reality was reflecting in everything and everyone around, almost like a dream that's awake in itself. Realising this, I could soar and hop in my energy flow like I was liberated in the acknowledgement of connectivity. I then breathed and told myself to relax throughout the exciting and weird visions. My body felt uncomfortable with

Ayahuasca entirely online—my whole body felt like jelly when I tried to stand up. I quickly laid back down and realised I needed more time to deepen into the experience.

I began to sink deeper and deeper into my bed as I laid back down again. Wilfully letting go of my struggle. I released everything: the sounds, sensations, and thoughts. I began to float through my deep inner body-knowings. As I was flying, suddenly, my gut area began to have waves of sickness. Just then I began to hear someone being sick in the room, and miraculously all of my queasiness went away. I recognised at that moment, this first-person to purge had done so for the whole room. I thanked them with a realisation I didn't yet fully understand. I finally did not feel so uncomfortable in my body and was able to sink further into the experience now.

In that moment, my mattress was the most comfortable embrace of mother earth, and I bathed in her warmth. I felt so soothed and cared for by life at this point that all of my previous discomforts went away. Sinking deeper and deeper into this relaxation, I began to see a myriad of eyes watching me from within. It was an all-knowing 'Presence' that seemed to be watching me from all around. I felt that I was being tested by this presence to make sure I was ready to sink even deeper into my experience. If fear or worry popped up in my mind, a horrible image would arise that directly corresponded with the feeling of this thought. When I allowed myself to be at peace and remember that I had nothing to hide, the experience became one of love and bonding. I could feel Ayahuasca looking everywhere inside my whole being—into the very depths of my soul—and relaying to me what she found there. Somehow, I felt ready and prepared for this, and the whole experience turned into fractals of sacred geometry all around me when I opened my eyes.

The music playing throughout the ceremony sent me into an utterly transcendental state. I was able to connect with this beautiful, uplifting music in a way I had never experienced before. This came after I purged something, mostly internally. Having chosen a spot next to the garden, I could face and turn three trees that stood in front of me out in nature. Some moments in this room full of people became intense for me.

Rather than freaking out, I focused on nature—a wholesome relief. As I watched with my eyes open, I began to see connecting geometric shapes everywhere. Everything seemed to be communicating with me in some miraculous way. I gazed into the trees and realised they had faces, a countenance and consciousness all their own. One, in particular, began speaking to me. The trees' words were of great comfort. It seemed they were initiating me into this my experience with great love, care, and support.

Though I could hear many other people in the room having more difficulties than I, thanking Mother Ayahuasca, I felt tremendously grateful for the whole experience. As I began to notice my throat buzzing, I felt called to sing along with the beautiful music that happened to be playing in the room at the time. My ego eventually got the better of me, and the medicine showed me this directly. I began to get increasingly annoyed at the other people in the room who were being very loud, shouting, screaming. I had the urge to run away from all of the commotion, but my body still felt a little wobbly and ungrounded.

Suddenly, I heard some deafening screams from someone across the way. Although they seemed to be very scared, my ego could not handle how selfish they were being by choosing to be so loud. In this rage, I turned to where the noise was coming from and said out loud "really?" I felt uncomfortably entitled at this moment and realised that I was not respecting others with my behaviour. I realised that just because I was personally allowing Ayahuasca to do her work through me in relative peace, others could not easily let go. Many of them were seemingly purging their 'demons' first before they could go more in-depth with Mother Aya and their own souls. This judgement of mine was clearly my own demon that I had to face. After receiving many downloads about how I had been this judgemental in previous experiences, I began to calm my ego down and realise I had some work to do.

Though the loud sounds did not stop there, suddenly, a man next to Ethan began to make thunderous grunting sounds. It sounded like he was about to do something violent, and I was immediately on extreme alert, ready to pounce if this stranger would do anything to Ethan. Luckily for me, the shamans were there in time as he began to rock from side to side frantically. As these female shamans tried to reach out their hand and use their voice to calm this man, I saw through his feeling body at this moment, which interpreted the shamans as some kind of monsters. He screamed and went from being extremely angry to then being very scared and fearful. I learnt a valuable lesson from witnessing all of this. It taught me that even if you have angels in front of you, you can mistakenly perceive them as demons if you are lost within your mind or emotions. Eventually, he calmed down, and by the end of the ceremony was giggling like a happy child.

The rest of the ceremony felt pretty blissful, and my only purging involved yawning. I had eventually managed to stand barefoot on the grass, and it felt amazing! I found myself bowing to the trees and plants and stroking them with my hands in a nurturing way. As I stood in nature, I felt more connected to all of these people in the room, it was as if I had found my root again. Throughout the ceremony, shamans would walk by casting tonnes of sage smoke into the air as they did. Their footsteps sounded like the beat of a drum, and it was a steady feeling that would envelop me when they walked by.

Some souls were particularly lost on this first night, a few even coming close to my bed and wandering aimlessly nearby, which particularly bothered me. Though once the shamans went into the room, I felt grounded once more, and my anger turned into a release of fear. By morning we were warmly greeted by the lights being switched on, and being told to come to the central area to talk as a group. There was a distinct feeling of grogginess in my being but certainly a sense of communion as we sat listening to others' experiences. I felt altogether unsure how much time had passed. My sleep that following night felt like a continuation of the ceremony, each dream carried intense visuals and metaphors.

The next night, the ceremony happened to fall on my 24th birthday. This also happened to be the peak of the astrological Lions gate. After my first night's experience with Ayahuasca, I felt more confident than ever to take part in another ceremony. We spoke to some people after our first experience with the medicine who had also had similar experiences of elevation and visuals. Many others though, had one of the most challenging nights of their lives, relaying their vivid stories to me in detail. I figured that my dark night of the soul experience years before this night had already initiated and liberated my consciousness. My previous dark night had shown me the shadows of my being, and this perhaps facilitated a more comfortable trip with Ayahuasca.

While I lay on my bed, waiting for the second brew of the week to kick in, I began to realise I could not have asked for a better birthday present. After all, I was surrounded by like-minded people close by me in this fantastic retreat. We were all there to do excellent soul work and make our ancestors proud. I felt a community spirit building in my being, and with it being my birthday, I somehow felt like I was the leader of this pack. As I began to feel the beginnings of my six-hour long journey with Ayahuasca come upon me, I could not stop yawning. The yawning felt terrific, and I remembered how it felt to be a lion yawning next to a sublime sunset. The more I stretched, the more I felt this spirit animal imbuing me with confidence and courage. The feeling was euphoric and empowering. I sat in full gratitude, for being a part of this fantastic pack of souls. The silence amongst us felt like one of my best birthday gifts yet.

In this sacred space of silence, we were expressing our true, authentic selves energetically. As opposed to communicating with words, it felt like everything we had to offer of ourselves was through our expression in silence. This made more sense to me than the majority of conversations I had ever had. It felt as though I was finally able to rest in my feminine energy that was receptive as opposed to reactive. I began to laugh at the notion of being a lion again as the sensations took over my whole body. I entirely vibed with my Leo energy on this lions gate night. I felt an invincible energy force come over me, which felt like bliss, balancing my masculine and feminine energies entirely. Once again, I began to sing along to the music, feeling so incredibly comfortable in my own skin.

Halfway through this second ceremony, I decided to get up and wander around instead of lying in my bed. The moment I tried to place my feet on the ground, they felt flimsy, like jelly again, and I could not walk. I realised that I had to give my body a few moments to ground into my feet properly. I had sent all of my energy into the head where the visionary experiences were taking place. As I stepped off my bed and onto the dry grass, I heard all of nature speaking to me in sync. I lifted my head to the sky and saw shining stars that filled up my entire vision. These stars were the most beautiful array of bright, glistening eyes. I gasped in astonishment and felt as though the sky people were watching all of us from galaxies away. I had so much love for nature at this moment, the shining stars had never looked so brilliant or so close before. As I peered closer, I could feel them staring right back at me. Each star looked like faces all watching in unison, and collectively they were viewing everything that was taking place in the ceremony. The astonishing nature of this realisation felt almost too colossal for my mind to fully comprehend at this moment. I climbed onto one of the hammocks outside, and promised the stars that I would connect with them some other time more fully. As for right now, I simply wanted to take in their beauty as I knew, I still had some internal work to do.

After another revelatory night of profound experiences, I was strangely feeling exhausted. As I sat waiting for the third ceremony to begin, my whole body felt drained and low in energy. The journeys would go on into the early hours of the night, and classes happened to start early the following morning. We often did not feel well-rested which was the only drawback to the experience. I felt like I was using the last strains of energy I had left in me, though somehow, I kept powering through the experience. After drinking the brew, the effects took hold sometime later, and I began to feel a little discomfort at this time. This time Aya began showing me the many relationships in my world, as they all flashed before my eyes. I heard Ayahuasca correcting me on some of my beliefs about these friends or family members. It felt like being put in my place gently many times. Ayahuasca gave me advice, especially during a review of past experiences and relationships with others. She told me "not be so judgemental" and focus on myself and my mission instead.

Unfortunately, I was unable to heed this advice immediately as I became increasingly annoyed. Some people continued to speak out loud even though they had been instructed not to. I perceived this to be arrogance on the part of others, who needed constant mollycoddling from the shamans. I saw how these adults were seemingly acting out childish behaviours but with rage, and I became worried that some of us would have to step in. The shamans were used to this though and had it fully covered. As I lay back down on my bed to go inward again, I felt more anger brewing within me. My body felt so uncomfortable, and now I felt like I wanted to scream. I wanted to run away from the room at this point. In fact, it felt like I wanted to run away from the whole world as I was 'agitated' by all of it. After what seemed like an eternity, stewing in this anger, I finally stood up. It dawned on me that I had been trying to run away from myself all this time. I tried to understand what I had been pushing away within me and began to hear some drumming coming from the main room. This grounding sound was a welcomed relief from my current thoughts, and many of us joined the shamans in their musical celebrations.

As I grounded into my body and feet again, I started to feel better, and a lot less angry towards everyone. I moved to the beat of the drum and allowed myself to sway in a serpentine motion with my spine. This taught me the importance of grounding as I have no doubt that I could have stewed in that anger all night if it had not been for Ethan gently whispering in my ears. He told me about the drumming next door, which I had not heard prior as I was so caught up in my own emotions. After spending some time grounding and dancing, I felt myself being drawn to the fire outside. I allowed my movements to flow naturally as I walked towards the fire pit outside, and I felt taller than ever. As I approached, I saw three other women around my own age, who all happened to be sisters. Sitting there with them, I felt a great synergy form between us.

Two of the sisters began to laugh hysterically with one another, and I could not help but laugh with them. It felt as though we had all come to the fire for the same reason. We each had taken a step back from the intense darkness going on in the ceremony. I felt the need to hold space for everyone now and actually enjoy the experience and this newfound freedom. This moment in front of the fire with these sisters felt sacred to me somehow. The light of the fire relayed a story to me of having had sisters of my own long ago in a past life. It felt so good to be part of a divine sacred sisterhood with these sisters, even if it was only for five minutes. I enjoyed this homely feeling immensely since I had always longed for a sister since being a young child.

The final and fourth ceremony was precipitated by a lot of fear and tears for me. I still felt so energetically exhausted and drained from the previous day, and my third ceremony had been a little bit more complicated. Many people had already purged so much. Including being sick and going to the toilet, but I still had not. This prospect made me fear that Ayahuasca must surely have something scary in store for me too. I had not done much purging in the same way others had. Though, I recognised that perhaps I did it in other ways, through yawning and sweating, for example. I could not help but worry that Ayahuasca was saving some dark visions of demons for me on this final night. My imagination and paranoia started to get the better of me, and I could feel that I was carrying an intense countenance, but could not help it. It felt as though it was the only thing I could do, to be authentic with how I felt. At one point, I attracted the attention of several of the helpers at this retreat, one in particular was the owner of the place. He took me aside to have a private word with me , clearly seeing that I was having some difficulties.

I told him that I felt so much anger inside of me. At the moment of saying it, I felt disappointed in myself for not being more grateful to this man since deep down, I respected this place immensely. He reassured me and asked me to think about the first time I had ever felt this way. As I thought about it, another part of me was wanting to look deeply into his eyes, as if I was trying to see whether the pure authenticity I had sensed from him all along was real. As I briefly looked into his soul, I sensed that this man was here to be of noble service to the world, and the next thing I knew he wished me goodbye. This short exchange was enough to make me tap back into my momentum again. I thought about what he had said and reminised to a root memory of having felt this way in the past. I could sense the profound work that so many people here were helping to facilitate in us all. I reminded myself to be grateful as this was an opportunity of a lifetime, though I still felt fearful of what was to come.

A few hours later, I cried on the bed silently to myself, waiting for the final brew to kick in once more. Finally, once its effects were taking place, I began to fall into what the shamans called "Nada." This Nada basically involved a deep, dreamless sleep in which a lot of healing is facilitated outside of our conscious awareness. I felt as though I had gone entirely unconscious. Though, at one point, I had a dark dream in which I was trying to help Ethan's stepdad who was suffering with cancer. After this Nada experience, I awoke to feel much more refreshed and welcomed the next round of visuals coming on. On this last night, we were being called to go and have healing performed by the shamans themselves. This first healing involved all of us women sitting in a circle in the centre of the room. Then two shamans blessed us with water, sweet smells, leaves and feather shakers. Individually, we received the healing, and the instruments were placed over our entire body in swift motions. I was incredible joyful to have finally gotten to this last ceremony and receive this healing, I could not help but sing along with the drumming and music the entire time.

For the remainder of the night, I allowed myself to enjoy the experience whole-heartedly, while occasionally having to face my shadows. Though, by the time we had finished the healing, I felt completely renewed and like my younger self again. Instead of going to our bedrooms before sunrise to sleep, this final ceremony lasted longer as we were allowed to drink as many cups of Ayahuasca as we felt necessary. By the third cup, I felt nauseous at the taste of the brew and was glad it would be my last time drinking it. After this final cup, I looked out into nature, connecting with the insects, animals and trees, and finally started to see the sun rising above the horizon. Watching as the sun rose in the sky was probably one of the most enchanting moments of my life. I felt an enormous amount of gratitude for the light and for existence during this sublime sunrise. I left my bed to have a final walk around the place as I knew the ceremony was coming to an end. It had gone by pretty quickly, and I wanted to make some last prayers to Gaia and Aya.

Walking around the small maze out in the garden, I realized my fears had been for nothing. My last experience with Aya had been harmless. I remembered back to the day previous to this last ceremony. Ethan and I had planted crystals all around the central area around the retreat. I heard a thank you from Spirit for having done this now, and proceeded to walk around the maze like my whole self again. I carried a gigantic smile and felt a mix of relief, amazement, and sadness that this journey had almost come to an end. Throughout these ceremonies, I had encountered many visions and channelings of information that would potentially take me a whole lifetime to unpack and decode.

Upon returning to my bed, I laughed uncontrollably at seeing three dogs that lived at this retreat, all fast asleep on my mattress. One, in particular, made me burst out laughing with tears. This pup looked so comfortable, lying on his back with his tongue hanging out. I realised at that moment that the dogs reflected how I was feeling inside, delighted and happy with where I was in life. I felt so full of joy and warmth, and I could feel how everyone who looked into my eyes noticed this glow. My whole body felt lighter than air, and my vision seemed brighter than ever. My eyes felt like bright lights, and as I looked all around me at the golden sun-kissed ground and sky, I saw bright rainbow wisps of energy in the grass and all around. It was almost as though crystals were within my vision. I assumed I was having the first taste of tapping into some extrasensory superpowers. More importantly, I felt a massive weight had been lifted from me during this whole process. Our sacred journey with Ayahuasca had finally come to an end.

SEVEN

New Beginnings, New Perspectives

∞

RECOLLECTING OUR PAST week's experience together while on the plane home attracted the attention of a few fellow travellers. We described to them all about the magical healing properties of this sacred plant medicine. However, many of them, just like us a few years prior, did not feel ready for such a journey. Most people had not even heard of Ayahuasca, especially in the western world, since this was an ancient practice of the native tribes.

One of the most significant realisations I came to after my experience with the medicine, was that I was a 'Highly Sensitive Person" known as HSP for short. This linked in with the knowledge that I was an Empath also, as they are both very similar. The loud noises I had experienced during the ceremony made me realise that I was intensely bothered by this kind of stimuli. Since childhood, I had often been easily overwhelmed by substantial sensory input, which was just one of the definitions of an 'HSP'.

During my experience with Ayahuasca, I explained to Ethan, I was able to not only see one of my past lives but also stay there for a while as a native woman. After asking Ayahuasca to show me my past experiences during the second ceremony, I saw a face in front of me, which continued to morph and warp at light speed. I couldn't make out each face very well, but I did recognise some faces which seemed more benevolent than others. It seemed Ayahuasca was showing me the faces of my past. Suddenly, I was transported to a remote desert-looking place with mountains. There, I found myself walking inside of a large yurt or tipi-looking building, along with what I sensed to be my grandmother. I realised that Aya was showing me my past life as a native woman, and the feeling of peace and tranquillity in this cosy home was extraordinary. I felt the feminine presence I had been longing for sat there next to the fire with my grandma.

As I saw myself living in my grandma's hut, I briefly confirmed to myself all of my previous notions about having lived as a native person. A part of me, my rigid ego, still doubted this information somehow. Though I realised what truly mattered was how I felt during and after the whole experience. This memory awoke something within me, and I trusted my instincts more because of it. I recognised during my stay there, sat with my kind grandma in a cosy hut, how much slower time seemed to move. Although I knew I was only there for a short time, there was something eternal about the experience. It was now an infinite living memory. I had somehow recollected this even with the amnesia that we are born into this life with.

Though, I knew some memories from past lives could actually hinder us in remembrance of them, a traumatic event, for example. This is why by the time we are children, many of us have completely forgotten about previous experiences, but the spirit within remembers. This memory must have stored in my genetics, I thought, as a blueprint of what peace felt like to me. I had previously been unable to see into past lives before, at least, beyond my visions. It seemed Ayahuasca was unwilling to show me any more than this. This sacred plant confirmed my belief in reincarnation in a whole new way. The overwhelming sense that I had lived past lives and would go on to live many more felt just as truthful as anything else did. I joked with Ethan that my whole experience with Ayahuasca was like that of spending time with a best friend. She was humourous and would even call me out on my childish thoughts or beliefs.

We felt so elated to have been able to experience and share this journey together. During the last day at the retreat, we remembered how one of our favourite shamans hugged us both goodbye and told us we would have beautiful babies. We laughed and wholeheartedly agreed with her, as we knew that someday we wanted children. The people we met there felt like fellow kin, and we hoped to be back eventually—once our wallets would permit such expenditure.

The whole experience had come with its challenges for us both. We saw our own shadows as well as our light. However, we continued to integrate a more profound understanding every day. Ethan told me how he saw a dark old witch release from my being during one of the ceremonies. We pondered over the many meanings this could have when suddenly I realised that throughout my childhood, I had several nightmares consisting of witches and scary old ladies. We assumed perhaps it had something to do with releasing these fears somehow.

All in all, we left Costa Rica feeling so much love, beauty and self-assuredness towards our path. Mother Ayahuasca had given us the gift of our souls back. We had experienced enough visions for us to delve into and decode for a lifetime. I had even managed to heal many past traumas and repressed anger issues that I was unaware of before this retreat.

One night, in particular, I recollected with Ethan, how it seemed I had experienced some kind of 'surgery' in my solar plexus area. This surgery was apparently not uncommon during the consumption of these plant medicines. It was stated that highly intelligent extraterrestrial beings were the ones performing this healing surgery. I did not see anything as I lay on my mattress during the experience. But I had the instinct that I was being worked on by something. It felt like prodding and lots of straggly feelings around my first three chakras. It was as though some kind of energy was being removed from underneath my skin. After this chakra healing had taken place, I noticed some dark discharge in my underwear the day after. When I asked Spirit what this was, I heard that it was something I no longer needed. Miraculously, I had been healed from a long-standing urinary tract infection, most of the pain I experienced in this region was finally gone.

Both Ethan and I recounted how we had witnessed some pretty crazy events during the Ayahuasca ceremony. We saw many different types of repressed traumas and experiences arise from people. Their healing journey had taken them on all sorts of routes to get to the other side of their pain and fear bodies. Some described how Ayahuasca had helped them to look inward to heal themselves during their purging moments. Others even discussed making contact with higher realms and beings of consciousness. We saw many people with deep wounds and illnesses be cured by the healing powers of this plant medicine. After my own sacred plant medicine journey, I noticed my anxiety dissipate by the time we had returned home.

We could not stop sighing with relief once we got back to Canada. What a fantastic experience it had been! Though there was still some unfinished business. After a massive argument between Ethan and I, Ethan let go of someone in his life as this person was causing problems between us. It seemed like Aya was still helping us to clear up any remaining baggage we had left in our worlds. I remembered feeling so loved and nurtured by mother aya that I carried this remembrance with me and was determined to feel it every day. I had no doubts as to the benevolence and incredible intelligence of this beautiful planet we inhabited. More so than this, I was also shown how Mother Nature could take care of herself. Everything is connected, even the people trying to control and dominate the world today, or the forces of evil. I saw that their souls were ultimately little children crying out for help, in the bodies of grown adults. Nature showed me that she was the real caretaker of this place, and would ultimately have the most say in what would pan out on Earth. If she wanted us to no longer be around as a species, we would be at the mercy of her.

She showed me that the 'negative forces' of this universe were merely bringing attention to themselves. All so that they may receive the love they so desperately long for within their soul. But only they can give it to themselves. I realised that everyone, at his or her deepest levels, is merely searching for the love of Source. Though many do not understand this and look for it in lots of different ways. During my Ayahuasca visions, I saw how the people in 'power' had nowhere near as much authority over life as they thought they had. Only Gaia herself and Father Sky had this kind of power and will, nothing and no one had more influence over the turn of events here than the benevolent spirits who take care of this place.

I was shown that ultimately, all of us are trying to get back to the love and bliss of unity that we sense is real, deep within our beings. This drives our deepest levels of understanding, and we are all trying to get back into harmony with our Soul's essence, our real source of life. Many of us have forgotten to remember and awaken to the Source of all that we really are. With the medicine still within our systems, I heard her words in my head speak to me again 'everything you need is within'. There was 'no room for doubt in myself anymore'. The experience was so profound that I discovered on a personal level how much we are all involved in this massive shift. An awakening of consciousness, taking place on the planet right now.

Ethan too, had experienced something very similar to me during his time with Ayahuasca. We both agreed that our leading roles in this life seemed to surround the idea of being a steward for the planet and sacred nature spaces. Ethan saw the intricacies of our universe and how it connected us all through a shared experience of awareness—each unique yet all profoundly interconnected. All experiences being woven together by the hand of synchronicity. We continued to recollect our experiences and uncover more memories of them and what they had revealed to us over the coming days.

One dark and cloudy morning, we got into another argument after noticing a picture of us in a frame had cracked while we were away. We wondered if this trying to send us a message. Perhaps there were still areas of our own relationship that we had to uncover the shadows from to keep on growing in love as a couple. This extremely heated argument between us seemed to reveal lingering fears and negative thoughts about our relationship.

After several hours spent apart to think clearly about what we wanted, we sat down together and honestly discussed what we really wanted together. We were no longer in the 'honeymoon' phase, which meant we could no longer fawn to each others' requests. If we did not agree or felt differently about something, we had to be honest with each other if this relationship was to be forever. After this well needed straightening out between us both, we began to make healthier lifestyle choices as a part of a new plan to live well. We adopted more of a vegetarian/vegan diet and began to practise yoga, meditation, and ritual exercise as often as possible.

The day had finally arrived for me to start my new job as an online English teacher. I had made sure I was well prepared previously by buying lots of props, making flashcards, and other fun things for kids. Having found new confidence and experiencing less social anxiety, I found my first day to be a success. I even managed to remember some of the beginner's Chinese that my new students were teaching me. Again, I realised how synchronicity had played an enormous role in my current circumstances. It turned out I was finally putting my degree to good use, and had many years previously visited China to learn all about this ancient culture. These experiences helped me to feel less of a culture shock and more confident in being these students new English teacher.

After several months of working with this online company, I felt stable in my income but not so much within my being. Teaching kids from a country twelve-hours ahead meant waking at four a.m. every day. The most fantastic parts of my day were catching the sunrise before lessons. With this new sunrise ritual, we developed a healthy morning routine which would stabilise my energy even more. I needed this extra confidence boost every morning because the job began to weigh on my soul after a while.

I became much more interested in Energy Healing during my time off between shifts and started to research it fanatically. After learning many different energy healing and energy medicine techniques as empaths, we decided we had to make them a part of our everyday routine. Every morning we would perform energy healing techniques on each other to tune into our bodies and strengthen our auras. It was miraculous that in just five minutes of practice every day, I noticed how much more calm and patient I was with the children. This even transformed one of the teaching challenges I was having. I could finally get some of my students to focus over a computer screen, not such an easy task as one might believe.

For all the hard work and synchronistic gifts we were receiving, I still struggled with deep angst within my being most mornings. It felt as though I was still not truly free the longer I stayed in this teaching job. Even within this new life that we had created for ourselves. It felt as though we were chained to the obligation of making enough money to survive still, just as the entire population too were chained. I hated almost every second of my younger school life. So I had promised myself that if I ever felt trapped again like I did at school, I would give myself the freedom to leave and find something else. Ethan too felt this same angst as he had been through countless jobs, searching for something that gave him joy, but he had still not found his 'calling' yet. We both knew it was close though, we just had to keep doing what we could, praying and remembering to spot the synchronicities in everyday life.

One day, after a long morning with my students, I was feeling somewhat demotivated at the thought of teaching English for the rest of my life. I decided to print off lots of beautiful pictures of nature landscapes to take my mind off of these troubles. Adding them to a shared vision board Ethan and I had in our bedroom. We knew about the power of our thoughts, paired with our feeling body and how it could potentially manifest our dreams. I had no doubts in this method as I had seen time and time again how the 'Law of Attraction' worked in my world. Sure, there were often many other factors that determined what would manifest within our life. In the least, we knew that having a clear focus for our dreams and goals was tantamount.

Luckily, Ethan and I shared a vision: we both wished to live a fully self-sustained life, especially one that focused around a secret garden. We would grow our own food and take care of animals. Another dream of ours involved having a sacred tent, yurt or tipi, which could house atleast eight people. There we would be the facilitator of meditation journeys, energy work and group healings. This shared passion had already manifested a beautiful secret garden where we currently lived. We watched how the garden grew more bounteous every day. The wildflowers and plants attracted lots of new critters and creatures. This was especially astonishing since we lived near a busy main road and had a loud train behind our home.

Most of our time was spent in our secret garden, since we both worked from home. My connection to nature grew stronger every day, and I noticed that more and more animals would approach us. These animal meetings seemed to correlate with the self-work and effort we were putting into becoming better people. We knew we were here to do good in the world and spread love as Lightworkers. So we continued to learn how to communicate with Mother Nature and what she needed since we knew that one day this would be our main dream job.

We had begun looking into EarthShip-style houses, which were cosy, spacious and good for the environment. These 'EarthShips' would be a thing of the future we concluded. Built-in a way that was a lot less damaging to Mother Earth. With everything potentially degrading the planet right now. We had to think of new solutions to live in harmony with nature. Otherwise, we might not survive the damages to the ecologies we were collectively doling out. Every day we shared our dreams with one another and fantasised about our future home and secret garden. It had become a constant reminder of joy and helped us face our fears. By letting nature grow in her entirety, our bodies and minds would flourish from the giving and receiving of garden goods sewn by our own hands.

We currently lived in a cosy attic space, which served us well as a couple. However, we began to resent the constant city noise and had minimal lighting or headroom living in an attic. One day after discussing our monetary concerns, we discovered that Ethan would have to go bankrupt to move forward and have a fresh start. On the way back from a bankruptcy meeting in town, we decided to go to the local charity shop, to see if they had anything available for our garden to cheer us up. We came home so chuffed to have been able to snag a beautiful black and white stone table. We placed it in our prized back garden space and began to feed the birds from it every single day. This brought even more animals to our back garden, which delighted us to no end.

In fact, going out to feed the birds every day turned out to be one of our favourite things to do together. Our dreams of a secret garden began to turn into reality before our eyes. The new feeding station not only attracted birds but a variety of magnificent furry creatures including chipmunks, racoons, a family of squirrels, and even three bunny rabbits. With some of the downsides to living in the attic, we realised it had a flourishing garden which had become our safe haven and sanctuary. When the summer came, we allowed this garden to grow in her full natural, wild way—and it became the most magical space for us.

NEW BEGINNINGS, NEW PERSPECTIVES

EIGHT

The Journey to The Sun

∞

ONE EVENING I sat down to listen to a voice message from a girlfriend about discovering her Lemurian past life. At precisely the same time, I also received another note from someone I had not heard from in a while. She detailed how she had performed a ritual to discover past lives. I took these messages as signs from synchronicity. The time had come to perform a ceremony of my own to look deeper into my past experiences.

For the ritual, we placed two yoga mats in front of our crystal altar, dedicated to our dreams and goals, and we set the intention that it may protect us on our journey. We then blessed our room with some sage to clear any stagnant energy away. This created a sacred space for the recall to occur. Next, we darkened the room and chose some Native American drumming music playing in the background. With nothing but candlelight between Ethan and I. We then both set our intentions very clearly. We were going to journey into a deep meditation to potentially uncover who we had been previously. We sat in front of our altar for a good twenty minutes giving gratitude and using affirmations. Chanting to get our resonance to vibrate at a faster pace. Eventually, we laid down and allowed our bodies to fully relax onto the mats.

The whole process felt very sacred, and this time, I was determined to be courageous and not afraid of what I might uncover there. Previously, I had tried to delve into past lives through meditation. I had even been given the ability to travel to the sun. But for some reason, I had been too afraid to visit the sun, and the vision had stopped entirely. If the opportunity arose again for me to travel to the sun, this time I would take it, I thought. Once I made my intentions known from within, I suddenly felt the presence of an angel, ancestor, or spirit animal with me. Though I could not be sure which it was at this time, I knew that I was going to be guided during this journey. All I had to do was keep my thoughts positive, relax and not become afraid of the unknown.

Ethan and I began to let our breathing guide the way for the rest of the journey. I felt grounded and began to breathe deeper to the drumming, relaxing into my third eye. As I did, I saw my spirit animal, a winged lion, arrive at my back door outside our attic space. I watched myself astrally release from my body momentarily and walked down the stairs where my spirit animal waited for me. Many of my recent dreams had been filled with cats. In some of them, I had been afraid that the animal would kill me. I synchronistically remembered an ancient shamanic teaching that spoke of spirit animals sometimes chasing you in your dreams to communicate.

This time I felt my loyal connection to this cat energy and greeted my spirit animal with open arms. This meeting felt so much more comfortable and laid back this time. I was calm and felt a deep love in my heart for this animal, almost as if I was greeting a long lost friend. After stroking and hugging her, I climbed on her back, and we immediately took flight. We flew past many high clouds in the sky, over the top of a beach, and passed over an expansive forested area.

At the edge of this forest, next to a beach, stood a cosy, perfectly sized house. It had luscious greenery growing all along its walls and lots of flowers around its windows. I gasped as I recognised this place with a deep knowing in my heart. This a quaint-looking house, I knew, was much bigger on the inside than it looked from the outside. The first time I had ever visited this house was almost five years prior when I had been working at a retail store on the weekends while studying at university. During these long days of serving customers behind the till, I would often daydream about this magnificent ancient home. It had every room you could think of, and I spent many long hours there in my mind.

There was a whole room for each sacred element. The living room, for example, was dedicated to the fire element. It had a cosy fire and lots of warm orange and purple tones. I sat on top of some incredibly soft rugs in front of this homely heat. All the while being mesmerised by the roaring fire. This room was a place to venture into the warm hearth of your own soul. The welcoming space was used to reflect upon oneself in sacred silence, and enjoy warm brews on a cold day. The next room was dedicated to the element of water, and in it were several different bodies of water. The purpose of this room was to manifest your intentions and desires while communicating with the essential oil pools. There were many statues of Buddha and other ascended masters there too. You could use this room to rest in the pools of tranquillity and meditate while levitating with the waters magical powers. It even had a little corner in the room dedicated to ice beverages, where you could make delicious fruit drinks or ice-lollies on a warm day.

Next was the gigantic library, which was dedicated to the element of air. Within its secret tunnels throughout the library, you could find cosy spots to develop your intellect by reading some of the most sacred texts of our times. High ceilings and decorative sculptures adorned this welcoming space. Through a secret doorway in the library, the next room was the element of Aether, dedicated to the arts. Within it was a gallery of amazingly intricate mandalas and psychedelic murals. I would often visit them to reflect upon my creativity and passions in life. The secret garden behind the house was of course dedicated to the element of Earth. The most splendid colours from fruits and flowers covered the lush greenery all around. A beautiful path of clovers led to an archway, and beyond the arch, lived all kinds of creatures. From faery folk to cute critters of all sizes, they all loved this magical place as much as I did. They weaved their way in between the many fruit trees, eating all that grew there in abundance.

I remembered how I used to come to this place in my daydreams at work, and how it always left me feeling rested and more joyful of spirit. I began to realise how this visionary, imaginary world of mine, was a personal journey I frequently took to find love in my heart again. This ancient home of mine was somehow elevating my consciousness by being in the mere presence of it. Visiting this place was a unique tool I could use to improve my mood on particularly tricky days, I thought. As my spirit animal and I both entered each exquisite room to this house, I felt a familiarity and safety here that I had never felt in any other place. My lion friend had now turned into a small cat, and she jumped up into my arms while we cuddled by the fire with some warm drinks. Once I began to feel more relaxed and calm, my cat friend told me that I was to go down the stairs of this house to the basement. I asked my spirit animal if she could come with me, and she led me down a black spiral staircase, which finally ended at a portal. At this point, I knew my furry friend could go no further, and I knew it was up to me to choose strength and courage and step forward into the unknown.

Upon entering the Milky Way looking portal, I saw an invisible path before me, which I happened to be standing on in outer space. I could see stars all around me, and either side of this hidden pathway was an infinite number of doors. I felt my heart beating with excitement, and suddenly I noticed the Goddess Hathor approaching me. I smiled mightily and greeted her with much warmth and relief. Hathor had come to me for the first time just before I had started working at the retail store. One night alone in my university dorm, I began researching in-depth the Egyptian gods at the time. Upon finding Hathor, the Goddess of Love, I felt such a connection to her that I designed my own Egyptian tattoo that night.

I resonated with Goddess Hathor because of my astrological Leo roots. After doing a natal chart in my younger years, I discovered my ruling planet was actually that of a star, Sol, Earth's sun. I had always felt a profound connection to the sun. Hathor, too, was known as a sun goddess and wore the suns emblem upon her head. I decided that I wanted to incorporate the symbols of the sun and of love into my tattoo. So I drew the sun circle, resting upon the two crescent moons, representing the knowledge of intuition. Then I sketched the two famous wings of Hathor's headdress on either side to represent the flying capabilities of the third eye. The final sketch showed this Egyptian emblem resting upon my two Leo glyphs. I had it tattooed onto my arm the following day so that every time I looked at it, I would be reminded of this connection to the Goddess of Love and to my courage. I would also be made aware of my brightness connected to Leo, which instilled a sense of confidence in me.

Hathor spoke to me within this realm of past lives now. She told me to walk along this invisible path and choose a door. As I began walking down the trail, I could hear the sun beckoning me as I began to see its shimmering rays beyond in the distance. It seemed so far away that I decided I would have to run to reach it. A moment of doubt overtook me as I began to wonder what

I would find once I reached the sun. Just then, the sound of the drumming music coming from my attic bedroom changed to that of a faster tempo. I took this as my cue to start running along the path as the beat of the drum roared more intensely. I felt so immersed in this drumming that I began to sense my angels and ancestors clapping me along now.

The journey to the sun turned into an exhilarating experience as I began to dance while running towards the light. I felt like all of the help I would ever need was with me then. I felt utterly confident, running along this imperceptible path. I finally arrived at the sun, it's warmth blazing my entire body in a nurturing embrace. As I began to step inside of this magnificent solar body, the drumming started to fade. Having entered wholly into the sun now, I was met with complete darkness. I felt a moment of fear until I realised it was up to me to direct my thoughts. I commanded "let there be light," and so there was, and the darkness faded away.

Before me, I saw a campfire with six people sat around it. As I approached them, I felt so much love and warmth for them all, that it began pouring out of me like rain. I melted into the comfort of love as I looked into the eyes of each and every one of them, simultaneously remembering how they had played a role in my soul's journey. Each one was a part of my soul group and had been with me through many lifetimes. The first person I approached was a native-looking man named Leo, and I realised he had been my brother in a past life and was still continuing to protect me in this life. Next, I met a light looking Celtic woman with blonde hair. Her name was Luna, and she spun me around in a circle reminding me of the fun and play we had experienced together in a past life. We quietly spoke together about how she had remained connected to my soul this whole time.

Then I met a red-haired woman, who seemed very down to Earth to me, and I recognised her as having a great deal to do with my most recent past life. She had been a simple housewife during an earlier century. Though, her heart and integrity were like that of a queen. As I met the remainder of my soul star family, I recognised a deep loving bond between us all. We danced around in a circle together, singing to the fire. I felt my connection to the community restored. I finally felt truly understood here and thoroughly at home within a group of people. I was told before leaving that I had still yet to meet two others from the soul group who were currently away on a mission.

I smiled at all of them and promised to be back. Finally, with a weary heart, I set on my way back out of the sun. The whole experience with them had been entirely uplifting and joyful. Hathor greeted me on the other side of the sun and told me the time had come to choose a door. As I began looking at the doors walking past them all, I felt overwhelmed with choice. Some were dark and battered, some were beige and natural-looking, others had bright colours on them. One, in particular, stood out to me, and as I looked at this door, Hathor cautioned me against entering.

Somehow, I already knew why Hathor cautioned me against this particular door. I knew that whatever I would have to face inside, would require a lot of strength. A deep pain of abandonment lay there. Seeing that I was very nervous about entering, Hathor began to perform reiki on me, and this helped calm me down a lot. Once I was fully relaxed in my body again, she told me that if what I was seeing became too difficult, I could instead visualize being sat in front of a screen. Almost as though I was watching my past life from a movie theatre. I told Hathor that this was exactly how I wanted to see it and asked if she would join me in this theatre. She agreed, and we both entered through this sparkling door to find a dark movie theatre with a massive screen in front of two seats. As I watched the first few minutes of my past life, I began to realise that this was one of my most creative and prestigious lifetimes.

I saw my sister of this past life and me inhabiting a whole planet to ourselves. I saw how our Father, a great god, had assigned one half of the planet to me and the other half to my sister. I watched how we would have constant sibling rivalry between us over who was the most skilled or creative when it came to building our own side of a planet. I was amazed to see how we were able to perform rituals involving the breath and strong focus, which allowed us to conjure up enough energy to build mountains with our very hands. I watched how just a few swift motions of drawing my hands up from the Earth to the sky, made a mountain appear before my very eyes. Our lives seemed creatively free in this place. We were wholly dedicated to co-creating with nature and performed songs and dances together upon our corners of the world. We were building this planet alongside one another for a future civilisation.

During the vision, I saw how I created a forest and how I strolled within it. Year later, I greeted many of the newborn animals there. Many of which were being seeded by a beautiful crystal device I carried with me. As I got to the other side of this forest, I came to a clearing and found my sister sat upon a giant swing facing a mighty cliff of stones and moss. The rain began pouring down on these rock faces now. The trickling sounds of the water dropping into every crevice made the most magical, calming sound that echoed throughout the whole forest. As keepers of the planet, this place was where we would often meet together. This would usually involve other council members from our galactic family too. I noticed my sister looking melancholy as she stared off into the distance. Once she heard me approaching, I observed that she was not carrying her usual exuberant energy.

"Eviael, what's wrong?" I interrogated her worryingly.

"Our father has just spoken to me. He has ordered us to go to the planet Earth and help the humans and assist their awakening,"

Eviael replied in a monotone voice.

"Then we must go, must we not?" I said somewhat shocked but determinedly.

"Perhaps we must not!" Eviael exclaimed.

"What are you talking about?" I asked.

"What if I want to stay and carry on living the life we have built for ourselves here, Alethia?!"

"I understand, Eviael. But you knew before we came here that Father had many plans for us, some of which involved going along with change. We knew that if we were to be granted the power to fulfil any of our dreams, we must be willing to go with the flow of our responsibilities," I stated in reflection.

"What if they come and try to take over our planet, or even worse, destroy our planet while we are away?" Eviael spoke solemnly with tears in her eyes.

"Maybe that does not have to happen!" I proclaim. "What if one of us stays here to guard the planet until the other has finished their mission on Earth?" I suggest.

"Well, I guess I already know which one of us is staying and which one of us is leaving," Eviael looked longingly at the forest once more. "What if I lose you, Ally...? What if you lose your way and cannot get back home?" she asked with concern.

"I won't. I will find the way back to you, dear sister" I said determinedly.

As we hugged each other goodbye, I heard Eviael communicating with me telepathically reassuring me that she would always be just a heart's call away. I wiped away my tears, knowing that even worlds between us could not keep us from helping each other. Before the movie had finished playing, I turned to Hathor and asked why I had been given these amazing abilities in a past life. She told me she did not know and that I would have to visit Sacred Spirit if I wanted answers. Suddenly I began to beam up and out of the movie theatre and found myself in a very light place. I seemed to travel along these luminous tendrils before reaching the centre of the Sacred Spirit of All.

Without hesitation, I asked, "What makes me so special that I could create worlds like this in a past life?"

Spirit laughed and said, "Don't you know how ancient you are?"

I began to think back to all of the doors I had passed to get there. So many of them shot through my mind that I could not begin to count. Instead of asking 'why me,' I told myself, 'why not?!' Perhaps I really could have experienced such things in a past life. I began to ponder about how many untapped skills were just waiting for me to uncover from a past life. If I had been a great artist or mathematician, for instance, then I could also tap into this right now in my current incarnation to some degree. I began to feel Hathor beckoning me to come back. I sat down to watch the remainder of my past life film. I saw how I was told by the galactic federation that I would have to incarnate on Earth as a human, and not watch over it as a lightbeing. This notion suddenly made me very uncomfortable as I knew this would take me even further away from my sister—and my memories.

I telepathically communicated these new plans to Eviael before I was about to reincarnate. Now though, I was plagued by an intensely sharp pain in my heart. There was no answer from my sister. I called out to her again and could not understand why all I could hear was silence. My Father then informed me that a most unfortunate event had occurred and some malevolent beings had caught wind of our plans to leave the planet. They knew that with me gone, my sister would be too distracted to stand on guard and they took their chance as soon as the opportunity arose and destroyed our planet. I felt so utterly hopeless. So much anger and sadness from deep within leapt out as a wail into the very depths of space. I was so mortified that I could even feel this same distraught emotion within me now, sitting with Hathor watching this past life from millions of years ago. Hathor tried to comfort me and told me that I was here to heal this ancient memory. To remember it, accept it, and to let it go.

We exited the movie theatre now, and I asked Hathor what had happened to my sister. She told me that her soul had come straight to me once she had died and that she lived within me, waiting to be reborn as my daughter. As she said this, I received tingles all throughout my body, and I let out another deep cry from within. I realised a deeper reason for having come to Earth now. I was determined more than ever to live a good life and to raise a family in my space of love. I still had so many questions buzzing around in my mind after this experience. I wondered who those beings were that came to destroy our planet, but I realised that all would be answered in synchronistic time. As I returned back the way I came, past the many doors, I realised I would have to come here again to uncover more of the truth about my past. Upon saying goodbye to Hathor and my old home, I spoke with my winged lion spirit animal friend, who told me that there was so much more to my story. More than I could comprehend right now, but that someday I would understand all of it.

We flew all the way back to mine and Ethan's little attic, and I awoke to feel extraordinarily calm yet so excited to tell Ethan all about the journey. Recounting the story to him, I felt surer than ever that I was exactly where I needed to be. I realised how much I had gained and healed from just this one past life viewing. Moreso, I realised that even though I had seemingly lost a part of myself, my sister, we would somehow be reunited once again, but in a brand new evolved way. This thought excited me and I could not wait to live out my mission on Earth.

THE CHRONICLES OF SYNCHRONICITY

NINE

Social Struggles and Healing Visions

∞

AFTER THE COLD winter had passed by, the welcoming hand of Spring was upon us once more. I was flying back home to England to see my family since I had not seen them in a while. As I stood queueing at airport security, I enjoyed the thought of being able to find flowers and birds in England that Canada did not have. I knew that with the coming Spring, lots of new species would be out as I walked the forest trails around my brother's home. I could not wait to hear the sound of silence once again, as they lived in the cosy English countryside. All we could hear for miles were the sound of occasional aeroplanes and children playing in the local primary school grounds. Farmer fields surrounded the area my family lived in, and I would be staying with them for the week. The forests and beautiful green hills reminded me of a place the elves would have once lived. It was not quite the secret garden space that we had back at home in Canada, but it definitely had its own charm to the place.

I spent a few days reuniting with many of my family members and felt more comfortable and calm around them than ever. Though I was still plagued by past memories of social difficulties.

My mind began to conjure up previous experiences with family, friends and acquaintances that had not felt so good. I thought about how I had previously had a massive flare-up of my social anxiety when it came to meeting someone important. It did not seem to make sense to me, I thought. I had already done so much healing with my inner child. I'd cleansed previous childhood wounds and traumas within my heritage and family line. I had done meditations specifically tailored to help heal past life traumas. Yet I still carried this social angst with me, especially around new people. I realized it was going to take more time for me to heal these social wounds. Logically, it did not make any sense to me, and my mind tortured me with how crazy it all sounded. I was afraid not to be approved or liked by people constantly.

As I dwelled even deeper into these thoughts, I began to feel out of control emotionally, and as though I was losing my mind. Maybe I was still experiencing some jet lag, I thought. I decided to put on my shoes and coat to go out into the forest. I walked up a hill next to the rustic stone walls that overlooked a beautiful yellow meadow of flowers. Feeling how these dark emotions were taking over my whole energy, my demeanour continued to grow in even more angst and confusion. After crossing an area in the top of the field, I came to a river that was surrounded by gigantic oak trees swaying in the wind.

Usually, this view was enough to make my mind turn silent, but even with this glorious landscape, I felt more alone and desperate than ever. After trying and failing to release my angst through tears and screams, I decided to try and think more positively about this whole situation as my negativity felt like it was starting to get the better of me. All of a sudden, I had a vision of what felt to be kindred souls all appearing before me in this hilly area. They had shimmering white outlines around their bodies, and I could barely discern what any of them looked like.

All I knew was that I was in the presence of very caring souls and as I wondered who these people were, I felt an immense weight lift off my shoulders as I greeted them with respect and love.

The leader of the group then stepped forwards towards me and spoke to me. Still somewhat new to this real-life vision taking place, I tried to readjust myself to receive whatever they were here to give to me. He then assured me that this here community was in fact, within me. During my loneliest times, he told me all I had to do was 'remember' their presence. He continued to tell me that I was to call upon them as often as I needed. They were connected to the nature in some way, and were here to provide support and comfort for me. This group of souls reminded me of how valued I was as a being on this planet. My mind suddenly shifted back to the thought of how immature I must have looked previously. I regretted my previous behaviour, but knew it had served a purpose. Though, screaming in the middle of a beautiful view was definitely not one of my most elegant moments.

Just then I heard a male voice inside my mind, beckoning me to come back into the present. He told me that these types of experiences were often the opening to visions, and would occur due to two factors. One being my willingness and readiness to ask and receive help. The second being the need for such contact to occur at the moment. There seemed to be a lot of information for me to decode and discern all at once. He then told me it did not have to be this way, that I did not have to go into complete emotional turmoil before having these visions and realizations about myself.

I could remember these people who loved me, as often as I needed to, and did not have to worry about what other people thought of me. I nodded and envisioned hugging each and every soul that had come to see me in nature that day. As I greeted and thanked them for being there, I had the sense to say to each and every one of them, "I know you." And as I did, they would each smile and nod back at me. They felt very angelic, and I began to wonder if I had just met the 'elves' that are so often credited with inhabiting these English hills. With the feelings these meetings come with, it's little wonder so much fantasy and storytelling arises from them. Perhaps many of the lands' fairytales are based on these profoundly satisfying experiences.

...

It had been almost two weeks since my short visit home to England, and I was still struggling with this long-standing issue that I was unable to come to terms with. My main concern had always been socially related, and I found that in most days of late, I was continually emotionally triggered by others. I would feel like crap some days, and would often find myself falling into deep emotional distress. I could still remember the words of these lightbeing souls that had come to visit me in nature that day. But for some reason, I could not shake the feelings of shame and fear. These days were filled with social angst and social inferiority more than ever. Perhaps I was finally releasing the years worth of social struggles which had been with me since my teenage years, I thought.

It felt just as painful in the present moment as it had all those years ago. I felt at a loss at not having a close group of friends that I had always longed for. On this particularly rainy and cloudy day, I curled up inside of our bed in the early afternoon and began sobbing to the very depths of my being. Ethan ran over to the bed and asked me what was wrong, trying his best to comfort me. I could hardly answer his question, I felt so sick of being in this place of turmoil, yet not knowing how to manage or overcome it. Instead of crying for another moment longer, I told Ethan I needed to have a nap, and I let my body fully relax into the bed. As I began to rest, I coached myself to release and let go of everything to Mother Earth and Father universe. This letting go made way for me to come into my body more fully now, and I sensed that I was supposed to do an inward energy healing on my chakras using my imagination.

As I visualized the rainbow colours of each chakra along my spine, I began to go into a meditation. Starting with the root, I sensed into my connection to Mother Earth's core. I began to visualize golden energy coming up from the very centre of the universe into my being. This golden energy travelled all the way up into my feet, legs and began to spin my red root chakra even faster. The feeling of stability and security was starting to open and grow within my being now. Breathing in deeply through my nose, I then visualized a beautiful orange light turning on in my second chakra, three inches below my navel.

As the energy from earth continued to rise up into this second chakra now, I began to feel more in touch with my creativity and playfulness again. Picturing myself painting a magnificent piece of art and dancing in a field full of butterflies. Breathing out through the mouth now, I visualized my third chakra as a beautiful golden yellow sun, spinning so brightly in my solar plexus. I felt my confidence and self-assuredness switch on within my whole being, igniting my deep passion for life again. Next, I began feeling into my heart centre and could see many different shades of green swirl around this energy centre as it began to pulse. I pictured each and every heartbeat giving me an abundance of unconditional love. Entirely opening my chest and sensing into a lighter auric field radiating all around me now.

Breathing deeply, I sensed into the many open and closed chambers within my throat. I pictured a soothing ocean or lake swishing back and forth, cleansing and clearing this area and opening the chakra. Helping it to become more open to truthful communication. After a while, I sensed my throat vibrating and felt ready to communicate clearly and coherently with the universe. The energy from Mother Earth continued to travel slowly up my spine and eventually reached my third eye chakra. This beautiful indigo coloured sphere grew bolder, spinning and shining brightly. All the while, I basked in this heightened perception and sense of groundedness. Finally, as this golden energy travelled to the top of my head. I then saw a violet flame crown begin to form all around my energy body. I felt united to my connection with Divinity through my earth and sky chakras. They were channelling energy from above and below, sending this throughout my entire body in a spiralling motion. The deeper I breathed, the more power this visualization seemed to develop. This new clarity of energy within my body allowed me to reset my thoughts. I carried inspiration with me now, as opposed to fear and confusion. My body felt lighter, more in tune with the present moment, and I begin to notice my mind wandering to the thought of communication again.

By the end of this meditation, I thought about how, as a young child, I had longed to meet my grandmother. She had tragically died before I was born. Just as her mother before hers did too. I would often ask questions to my mother about Grandma, though there was not much information my mum seemed to be able to give me. She did not talk about her much at all. All I knew was that I wished to connect with her somehow, and this very thought seemed to open a line of communication between us at that moment. Suddenly, I heard her voice in my head and saw her face very clearly, almost as though she stood directly in front of me.

"Hello, love." she said happily.

"Hey Grandma, is that really you?" I asked.

"Well, I am whatever you think I am dear," she said half-jokingly.

"I have so many questions for you, Grandma" I sighed.

"I know you do. Remember I am always here, you just have to open contact as you did today. But right now I am here to help you with something. Do you mind if I get us to visualize something together right now?" Grandma asked.

"Of course! I am ready whenever you are Grandma," I said with anticipation.

"Now that you are nice and relaxed in your bed, I just want you to explore your imagination with me for a moment. Think about all of the people you have ever admired as a potential best friend," instructed grandma.

As she said this, I began to instantly collect a list of people in my mind that I had come across in my lifetime. I visualized them standing in front of me in line. I remembered the friendly energy some of them embodied from their personality and faces. I had not met all of them face to face, but I chose certain people based on a good feeling about their energy.

"Don't worry about them having to be the perfect person all the time. I just want you to choose the person and one characteristic that you appreciated from them. They can be young or old, male or female. All that matters is that the energy you choose to see in them right now feels good to you," continued grandma.

I thought of everyone I have ever met, narrowing them down into a group of people I genuinely admired in some way. Finally, choosing a character from each that I found most endearing.

"Grandma, I want my friend or friends to have qualities like these," I said as I began listing them to her in my mind. "Loyal, wise, friendly, authentic, caring, strong, loving, charismatic, honest, open, appreciative, nurturing, down to earth, practical, and imaginative. These are the qualities that I have valued the most in people during my time here on Earth."

"Very good. So now you have an idea of all the qualities you wish to look for within a friendship group. Now, I just want you to take all of these qualities and imagine them pouring and spiralling down into human form. Creating the most perfect friend right before your very eyes. Visualize this person, carrying all of the qualities that you admire the most. I want you to feel your interactions together. What you are both going to do for each other in your worlds. Take all the time you need to really live each and every detail," she said lovingly.

I did precisely what Grandma said and began to envision this best friend and I roaming about our day-to-day lives. Acknowledging and supporting each other along the way, in both small and big ways. From this friend helping me with my work, to me giving them advice when they were struggling with something. The connection felt so smooth and comfortable like I was able to breathe full fresh air again. The energy felt light, and I didn't have to worry about keeping them in my life. Nor did I have to worry about offending them, we just simply understood one another. In visualizing my time with them, none of it was filled with judgemental thoughts towards one another's behaviour. Instead, it felt just like we were soul friends, we had each other's backs, and that was all we needed. We had fun together, adventuring, building, creating lots of new things in life, and the connection just flowed like water down a slow and steady stream.

"There, you see. Now that's the type of friendship you deserve. No more of this worrying about whether you make a good enough friend. Or whether other people are going to like you or not. Now you can see that it is possible to not only meet the man of your dreams, you can also meet the friends of your dreams, too. These people will understand you better than you can understand yourself sometimes. They are already out there waiting for you Kate, all you have to do is keep this easy, comfortable vibration you have now going. Eventually, you will find the friends you have been looking for all your life. It doesn't have to be so hard any more love, simply come to this place where you bring everything in life to light in the way that you see best," she said smiling at me.

"Thank you so much, Grandma. I love you. Is there anything I can do for you? Do you want me to pass on a message to my mum for you?" I asked longingly.

"Yes, dear. Tell your mother I never left her side, that I have continued to help her and be there for her ever since I left so young. Tell her I can see how much she loves her daughter and that you love her dearly too," she shared.

"You mean... you can see how much I love my mum?" I interrupted.

"Yes, of course," she smiled warmly. "Tell your mum that her daughter chose her to be her mother that night we saw the purple spacecraft in the sky together."

"What?" I asked, shocked.

There was a long pause between us before I continued.

"You mean to say that the spacecraft you both saw that night was me coming to decide who would be my parent in the next life?" I asked in astonished reflection, almost as if I knew this already.

"Indeed. But you already knew that didn't you Kate?" She said coyly.

"I wasn't so sure, to be honest, Grandma. And I'm still not. But that is pretty amazing! I did think that the whole experience sounded so riveting when mum first mentioned seeing a UFO years ago," I reflected.

"Yes, your mum would've been around the age of seventeen when you decided you wanted to be her daughter," she stated. And as if to provide one last piece of advice, she added, "I can see how dearly you love her, but make sure not to ignore her messages, ok?"

"Of course, Grandma," I agreed, embarrassed, knowing precisely what she meant.

I hugged her goodbye and felt like the whole depressive experience I had just recently gone through had been entirely worth it. Even more so, seemingly orchestrated once again by our dear friend Synchronicity. I continued to leave these visions feeling more of who I was every single time.

SOCIAL STRUGGLES AND HEALING VISIONS

TEN

Energy Healing Practises

∞

ONE SUNNY AFTERNOON, I stepped outside after having finished teaching my students. For some reason, I felt unable to positively bask in the beautiful summer sunshine. I realised that even with this job, I was still left feeling unfulfilled. After taking a few grounding breaths, I headed indoors to continue my online research around spirituality. After a while, I came across a new style of energy healing that I had never seen before. Excited, I began taking a course in this new energy medicine technique over the next several months. With this new practice in hand, I began to feel a deeper calling from within me to share my purpose with the world. I was getting very close to my soul's path and mission on Earth, and it was palpable. Whatever it was, I intuited that energy healing would play a key role in it—as well as Light Language, since I had continued to study linguistics.

I appreciated this new passion and interest I had discovered as it seemed so familiar to me. Both Ethan were practising energy healing on each other every day still. I would often feel a sense that I had somehow done this kind of energy work in a previous lifetime. This inspired new ideas and ways to help ourselves that we did not previously have access to before. We were able to develop more confidence in our energetic abilities with continued practise. Eventually, I realised that many people could benefit from this kind of information. After all, very few teachers acknowledge that everything in the universe is made out of energy, and thus the impact it has on the way we interact with the world. It was still hard for the majority of society to accept this notion since many were so focused on the material world.

Finding a way to practise energy healing had come through a synchronistic email. After clicking on the link, I listened to the women teaching it and instantly resonated with her. She had a wise grandma type of vibe about her and was clearly just trying to do good in the world. These classes spurned a whole new way of thinking for me, and after practising it many months later, I felt inspired to teach about it myself. This brought back my passion for my online spiritual website once more, as I felt a call to create a course for people. This course, I decided, would teach them all about energy healing for empaths. I figured that there were plenty of other people out there, very empathic and sensitive to this modern-day world, that needed guidance. I had been noticing great results in my own life from this work, so I distilled much of my knowledge into one course. I knew it would take me several months to complete, but I felt determined to try nonetheless.

The following morning as we stood outside watching the sunrise before my classes, I had an overwhelming sense of angst and frustration wash over me. I was feeling the pressure from my student's parents, as many of them would sit in class with their child. If their child got any answers wrong, some of the parents would often smack their son or daughter in response. This kind of physical abuse was extreme from my point of view, and I always battled over how to tell the parent to stop. After many occasions of this happening, I would instead, congratulate the child at and give them as much praise as possible for having tried so hard to answer the question. Eventually, this seemed to deter some of the parents and stopped this kind of abuse with their child. As a teacher, I felt the pressure to do well and make sure there were no mistakes. Because of this abusive response from parents, a lot of fear and performance anxiety built up in both my students and me.

When it came to learning, we will always make mistakes, I concluded during this time. In my opinion, this should not be punished, as such punishment did not make the child learn any better. In fact, I continually watched how a parent would hit their child, and the child would then become even more reserved and quiet, hardly wanting to participate in class at all. They would not learn as efficiently and instead refrain from answering in fear of their punishment. I seemed to be taking on some of these kids angsts during classes, and some mornings were filled with anxiety-driven thoughts. On this particular morning, as we stood watching the sunrise, I wept at the feet of mother earth, and an enormous scream arose from within my being. I realised I felt trapped again, just like I did as a child when I was forced to go to school, even though I hated it. At least now I could try and help these kids, I bargained. But my inner voice told me that there was so little I could do since I was across the other side of the world, literally.

During this time working as an online teacher, I trained myself to use my breath to stay calm and focused during lessons. I used the energy healing techniques to prepare for the day, and I made sure to zip up my energy with an intention every morning. Usually, something like, "I am a shining beacon of love, light and truth," or, "I am a pure and powerful channel of Love's expansion." During the actual lessons teaching children, I became aware of the fact that all I needed to focus on was my breath. I was no longer trying to fix the problems that would arise in either the parents or child's behaviour, as there was nothing I could do behind a screen. I did, however, make a point to show patience, perseverance, and understanding with the children. I even began teaching them how to use breathwork at the beginning of our lessons together too, which helped them feel relaxed and at ease.

Still, I noticed many of the parents wanted their children to be achieving something every day, so we spent the most time going through the courseware. Some parents did not seem to like their child 'taking it easy' during class time, which was understandable. Instead, I continued to teach by focusing on my own breath every few seconds. Breathing in through my nose, I began internally invoking words like, 'relax, tranquillity, and joy' to myself. Then, breathing out through my mouth, I began internally invoking words such as 'release,' and, 'let go.' These simple techniques did wonders for my mental health during some of the most challenging classes. Though, I continued to find myself less and less motivated when it came to teaching English as the days went on.

After this particular morning of having wept at the ground of mother Earth, Ethan decided to do something wonderfully kind and built me a new website. This was to go along with the brand new course we were going to create. He surprised me with this brand-new website just after my classes had finished. As I looked at the screen he was showing me, I saw some vector art of a woman meditating, and the words 'Empaths deserve to feel peace and freedom.' I began to really believe that my dream to be a spiritual teacher could someday become real. I felt this immense support and love coming from Ethan, as he made me feel much less alone in this simple act of kindness. This was the tipping point, which actually inspired me to start writing my course. I finally felt understood by somebody, and even supported in my dreams. This love was my biggest inspiration in life now, which was incredibly motivating for me.

The following evening we sat together enjoying a vape of cannabis in our secret garden. As the peaceful, energising effects began to unveil, I stood up and began to feel energetic dance movements flow through me. It felt like a type of yoga dance, as every action felt so in tune with what my body needed. Each movement of release felt euphoric. During these types of energy movements, I would allow the intention to arise in me to honour the environment around us at the same time. This type of co-creation with nature-space felt accepting. Moreso, this led to more energy channelling through my body. I was also inspired at the time to sing more frequently, which encouraged me to open my voice, despite the stress I had been feeling lately. I understood that these inspirations were more synchronicities designed to convey a message. I felt a deep knowing that I was on the path towards my soul's mission. At the beginning of each channelling, I would get different images or imprints of what type of spiritual empowerment was channelling through me.

One day would feel like I was channelling communication from some kind of energetic crystal-being, the next channelling might be that of a woman of the wind or one of the other elementals. Each and every moment was unique, and I never knew what might come through. All I knew was that by focusing on my breath and body at the same time, powerful energy was able to arise within me. Every moment felt as if I was healing, giving and receiving to and from the consciousness of everything. Though the feeling often differed, I felt an intense, free, feminine energy in its deepest essence every time. The atmosphere was of pure strength, which felt grounded and then elevated a deep feeling of royalty within me. After these experiences, I began to use light language to communicate with nature more often. It appeared as if many other types of consciousness were in communication with me as well since new ideas continued to form. My plan had stayed the same every day, ever since visiting the sun, and that was to connect more deeply with my Sun Soul Self.

On occasion, some daily concerns would begin plaguing us. But over the following months, I consistently realised how perfect Ethan was for me. Only when I thought back to a memory from my childhood, did I understand that he had sprung precisely out of my own dreams. Though, he was even more than I could have ever asked for. I would receive visions of how synchronicity had brought us together in so many more ways than I could explain.

As a child, I was extremely gregarious. I wanted to be an actor, a singer, and I did not let the mocking laughs or words of others deter me from being a confident young girl. I had a reasonably decent childhood, despite some issues with alcohol, abandonment, and physical abuse within the family. When I was around the age of ten, everything changed when my parents split up, and my mother decided to move away. Around this time, I lost all of my confidence and struggled to 'fit in' at school. Looking back, I realised that the lonely nights spent in my room at home had been a catalyst to imagine and dream about another world—one that I actually wanted to live in.

Alone in my room every night, before going to bed for school the next day, I would act out the character of a queen or princess. As the princess or queen of my imagining, I was trapped by people in a castle of some kind. Every night I would dream up the same male character, who would somehow get past all of the guards and come find and rescue me in my castle. I would often fall asleep to the pretence that my king or prince was right there with me every single night. He would hold me in the most loving, warm, embrace that sent shivers down my spine.

I thought about Ethan now, and the beautiful synchronicities and memories we had shared together so far. I realised as clear as day that he was the exact prince I dreamt up as a child. All of those long, lonely nights spent pretending I was not alone but instead with him. This prince, I realised, was here with me now, manifested as Ethan. He was the loving character that I imagined him to be all those years ago, yet so much more. He cared for me deeply and showed me this care on every occasion he could. Just like my prince, who spent hours talking to me, nurturing me, and giving advice about my school problems before going to bed. Every single night. He would always be there to comfort me, to tell me I was ok, and that I would forever have him.

Moreso, this prince would tell me that everyone who was mean to me was jealous of me because I had something special. This made me realise that being afraid of the bullies at my school was not what mattered. My relationship with myself was what mattered the most. Ethan reflected this prince as he had consistently helped me over the last two years of our relationship together. Always there to hold space for me during my down days. Even going out of his way to cheer me up and remind me of why I deserved to love myself and be loved.

• • •

New cycles of synchronicity and joy continued to come about as I created my course. Every day, I spent some time outside writing each module and deciding what would go under each one. The structure of the curriculum followed that of the elements, Earth (body), Air (mind) Water (emotions) Fire (will), Aether (spiritual connection). I spent long hours, writing, reading, recording and filming this course. All the while, trials and traumas began surfacing to be healed at the same time. The course was serving as a tool for my own healing journey. Even though I was creating it to help other sensitive people in the world dealing with anxiety.

As I looked into the shadows that kept arising in my being, I began to revisit past memories. I assumed they had already been healed, but they instead had resurfaced again—mainly my traumatic memories of younger years at school. My dreams and waking visions began to be filled with past images of me running away from school, which I had done often towards the end of my school years. This feeling, I later realised, was due to the panic attacks I experienced during that time. As a young girl, I was unaware of the terms 'anxiety', or 'depression' and so had nowhere to emotionally express this angst. I realised these painful memories were from me having felt so trapped and unable to deal with the constant overwhelm of school life. During my last school years, I was left with no friends or teachers who could understand what I was going through. As I came back to the present moment now, I asked the angels to help me heal the constant nightmares from school. Then I heard a voice tell me to do some inner child healing meditations with myself.

After hearing this, many long nights were spent opening up to Ethan about my painful memories that still haunted my consciousness. I meditated and used a ritual with cannabis several times a month to help me release any last vestiges of emotion trapped inside. This helped to delve deeper into the emotional inner child healing my soul had been calling out for all this time.

One night during deep sleep, I began to have another dream about school. As I walked the familiar halls, I noticed that I did not feel as anxious as I usually did in this usual place. I queued to buy my lunch in the cafeteria and shortly heard girls gossiping about me standing in the queue. I began to feel uncomfortable within the dream, noticing all of the eyes watching me. Completely unaware that I was dreaming, I begin to feel the same triggers of sadness and heartbreak arise in me once again. I overheard an ex-best friend call out some rude comments towards me as I stood ahead in the queue.

I continued to ignore them as I lined up at the food counter, trying to decide what to buy. Then, I was suddenly hit with a moment of confusion and fogginess as if I could not determine what I wanted to eat. Feeling the eyes of others on me, I made a quick choice and reached for some food. At the same time, a girl beside me snatched it out of my hand. Feelings of shame and embarrassment arose again as everyone started to laugh. At this point, I decided to leave the cafeteria. Yet, instead of running out of there with my head down as I so often would, this time, I kept my head held high while I scanned the room. I looked at these ex-friends in the eyes, just glancing at them with a calm countenance as I exited the cafeteria doors.

Even though this act was small, it was enough to give me a new sense of direction. I was finally beginning to feel less afraid of these past memories in dreams. So often these dreams would feature me running away and trying to hide. I would be alone in a room somewhere, praying that no one would come to disturb me. Not this time though. This dream was different. As I exited the cafeteria, I began to feel a wave of sadness wash over me. I burst out into tears suddenly but as I stepped outside the school I saw my secret garden there waiting for me. At this welcomed sight, I was able to breathe a deep sigh of relief. Even though tons of people were in my garden, I am blissfully unaware of them as I step onto the ground with bare feet.

After waking from this dream, I felt a new rise of confidence well up in me. For once, I felt like my dreams were trying to help me, guide me, and show me a better way. The way of nature's truth. I recognized how my present seemed to now be catching up with my past. The notion arose that I had finally done enough healing work to clear these hurtful memories and move on from them. After that night, my dreams at school became much more infrequent. Which was a massive relief since I had dreamt about it consistently for more than a decade. Something had healed in me, and it was due to the remembrance of coming back to nature and my secret garden.

The next morning, as Ethan and I watched the sunrise together, it happened to be a weekend. With no work to do, I was able to relax in the golden rays of the sunshine all morning. It was the most perfect sunrise I had seen in a long time. With vibrant colours and transparent gradients above me, I thanked mother earth and father sky for this new life I was now living. As I did, I relived the dream as I told Ethan what had happened that night during my slumber. The sun was high in the sky as the clouds eventually began rolling in after a while. But I magically felt a deep wave of peace and freedom caress me, something I had not felt since being a young child.

I too thanked the angels and ancestors that morning and continued my prayers of gratitude all throughout the day. I had been released and felt genuinely free from years worth of torture at the thought of my past memories at school. I remembered how bright my light had been as a child. How often I had taken the role of a leader, a storyteller, an actress, that my childhood friends would so often wish to play with me. Instead of thinking of all the times I lost face at the cruelty of others, I began to think about how courageous my younger self had been. Before I had let any of the troubles of the world torment me. I had always remembered to use my imagination to get out of uncomfortable situations in life. Now I realised it was my superpower, and I ought to do it more often.

Later that day, Ethan and I began to envision our perfect secret garden wedding together. We fantasised about how we wanted to bring all of our families together from opposite sides of the globe. We hoped to eventually host a magnificent celebration of love from the comfort of our back garden. Though we had garden space, we did not have indoor space to accommodate guests. It was our dream to show our family and friends what living in true harmony with nature looked like. To show them how we would sit outside with the animals every day in joy and equanimity. How we would grow our own food through this fantastic garden. We fantasised about how this sacred place in nature is the space of love in which our children would be born into. That night after having discussed our marriage all day, we decided to elope first, and then the celebrations of our wedding would come later in our lives. All we could afford was a simple wedding, which was more than enough for us.

THE CHRONICLES OF SYNCHRONICITY

ELEVEN

A Rite of Passage

∞

WE HAD BEGUN fitting more of the pieces of our synchronicity puzzle together with each day. Often, the days were filled with joy and beauty, with the occassional down days where I would forget to love myself. Everywhere Ethan and I would go together, we felt supported by one another, and we were often told of our compatible synergy as a couple. Some days felt like we could light up the room as it seemed we were a positive power couple with great synergy. Other days did not feel so glorious, especially when some social triggers would arise for me. This particular day had started as usual, with our daily routine and teaching classes. However, after scrolling through social media and discussing some issues I had surrounding friends and family, I suddenly felt deeply triggered by something, and it was so deep that I had to step outside straight away.

I placed my feet on Mother Earth, and as Ethan handed me some lunch, I could not eat a single mouthful as a deep feeling of melancholy took over me. I began crying hysterically and heard a voice telling me to lie down on the ground and give this feeling to Earth to be transmuted. It felt as though I was in an ayahuasca ceremony, purging sounds and wrenching this negative energy, out of my body. I had never heard these scary sounds come from myself before, and I realised that something was clearing from me. After some time purging in nature, I asked the question to my spirit guides "What happened to me?"

I was transported to a memory of myself at the age of about seven. I remembered one night waking up from a terrible dream, only to feel as though it was really happening. I felt extraordinarily timid, seeing three witches with a cauldron at the end of my bed. At the time, I did not have much spiritual awareness, though I could feel the urgency to stay as still as possible. Otherwise, it seemed, the witches would come over and kill me. Instantly, I recognised this night had affected me on a deep level as these witches were there to curse me instead of kill me. Somehow, just this simple realisation managed to clear the deep emotions I was experiencing out in nature now, and I began to feel as though the curse had been lifted through the simple act of me being aware of it.

This experience suggested I had got to the bottom of a deep wound surrounding the feminine part of my nature. I turned to Ethan once we had finished our breakfast and asked him if he would like to go on a walk. The next sequence of events turned out to be so beautifully orchestrated that I began to understand the duality of my emotions on a deeper level. After having witnessed me this way, Ethan showed some concern towards me, but I reassured him that I had understood the message. As we walked down our busy main road, we decided to go along the train tracks, something we had never done before because the train was usually running. This day happened to be a national holiday though, so we were free to walk the train tracks at our own pace.

As we walked in silence along these tracks, I felt the innate sense arise that we were 'going somewhere', in more ways than just one, and mentioned this to Ethan. Along the way, we made several stops, each time it did not feel like where we were supposed to stay, so we carried on walking. Eventually, after thirty minutes of not knowing where we were going, we tried to find a cosy space for us to chat about what had just happened. We came to a clearing and a pathway that led into a forest. We had two choices as there was a fork in the road. We chose to go left, and we happened upon a beautiful reservoir. We laughed and smiled at each other since we had not been aware that such a beautiful place was only a thirty-minute walk away. We had given up our car several months before as part of the bankruptcy, and so finding this place was a complete gem to us.

We walked hand-in-hand around this reservoir and found a secret path through some bushes. This led to a perfect spot tucked in some trees in front of the water. We were able to see a family of swans in the lake and could hear the wonderfully calming sounds of bullfrogs all around us. We listened to chipmunks too and got to see some muskrats building a nest for themselves. We basked in the silence of nature together. And I gathered my thoughts to let Ethan know what my purging had been about. I waited for the perfect moment to talk, as I felt no reason to rush anymore. All my life, I had felt so rushed in completing anything or in getting started on any project. But there was a higher vibrational energy that I seemed to be tapping into now, even after having had such dense emotions occur. This energy felt like having gained my power back, as I realised there was no sense to all of this rushing in the world.

As we sat together, enjoying the nature sounds that seemed to be whispering words of comfort in every moment. I finally spoke and recounted the messages and visions that had come to me during the purge.

"So...when I asked...after purging...whatever it was that I

said...?"

"What happened to me?" Ethan answered.

"What happened to me," I confirmed.

"I thought of younger me, I was in primary school, and I was in my bedroom. And there was one night where I woke up, and I swore there were witches in the room, and I was scared that they were going to kill me. So I just kept my eyes closed so they wouldn't kill me. There was three of them, and they had a cauldron. And... erm, what I saw just now is that they weren't there to kill me, they were there to cast some kind of spell on me. It was right around the time that a girl from primary school who I thought was my friend, started bullying me daily. I hadn't really been bullied before, and I started losing my confidence around this time. I remember asking my mum for guidance with it, but it was almost like the witch thing, it did something to me where I completely lost a part of myself, and I've been gaining it back recently. It is my cat self, it is my courageous self because what the spell was, and what I saw, is that it was there to take away my courageous cat self. It was there to make me forget my cat nature which is kind of a bit like my protector. And erm..."

"Well I saw her, she's cool" Ethan interrupted.

"What happened is that I... I subsequently went years and years not having that courageous cat self, that confidence from my Leo self just seemed to disappear. Because when I was in my younger years, my family and people at primary school would always sing to me, and I didn't know why, they would always say Katey, the white lion. Maybe it was a cartoon show I dunno, but it's always stuck with me for some reason. I would ask mum and dad, why do you say that? And I never got an answer about it. And um, what happened was that remembrance kinda went away, and going into high school. I completely forgot my courage, I completely forgot my confidence. I used to always be up on stage, and I would sing in front of anyone, but that dramatically changed when I got older."

Pause.

"Almost as though I was a completely different person. This energy was completely drained from me. So the pain that I released before, like wow, it was so guttural. I don't think I've adequately cried like that before. That cry was for all those years that I couldn't get in touch with that self. It had been there to protect me. I just took on all of the pain, the stuff that was given to me, and I tried to shove it down into the gut. Into the place where I had to release. And what's been happening these last few weeks is that cat self has been slowly returning to me, has been coming back to me, I guess I…"

"She's like a humanoid…cat …she's like a feline person," Ethan said.

"Yes. I um, I asked today to know how to… to feel like she's never gonna leave me again, because… How," I stammered, "how can I invoke her."

"Well, she's already with you," Ethan reminded me.

"If I need to invoke it, now all I have to do is say the words. Then she will be there. Whereas before, I didn't even know that she was taken from me with that witch stuff. So… what I saw… because I was asking, why am I so afraid of women, what is that? And I saw something about how there was a matriarchal thing, and I've seen the worst of what women can be. And it's to do with some evil witches of that time." I reflect.

"That's right. And they represent the dark side of our potential. Because you can also see the best of what witches can be, and that's what you are, you are the light side" Ethan shared in confidence.

"They were there to do their spell, now that has been given back to them. It's no longer mine, I've been able to release it. Release the pain that came with not having that part of me. Because really, even beyond a cat self, it was just a part of me, I lost a part of me. And I knew that. Because when I was growing up—and I tell this story all the time—I was the most gregarious person you would... you would meet," I share.

"Of course, because that's how the white witch is. That's the angel" Ethan confides.

As if to stand taller in my realisation, "I wasn't scared of anything, anyone, but that nightmare and the subsequent ones to follow was something deep to me... now I understand they weren't there to kill me physically, but to kill a part of me."

"Wow, a big heron, huge, just flew past!" Gasped Ethan.

"So that was the witch that I saw. When we were on ayahuasca. I think I must've seen your curse." whispered Ethan in remembrance of our previous journey.

"Hmmh, makes sense," I said.

"But how...I didn't know curses could come from... I thought they had to come from people on this realm. Cause they weren't of this realm, they were of another realm." I claim as I try to understand the odd circumstances around this experience.

"Well... more like they were of another timeline," said Ethan.

"Yeah, maybe and they came..." I began.

"As soon as you understand even a little bit about timelines, I mean we are dumbed down to the maximum as a human culture, we know nothing," interrupted Ethan.

"Oh wow, an eagle." We both said in unison.

"Well here's the thing, the reason why you've been suppressed is that they know your power. They understand the power of love because love always overcomes any evil. Because evil is a distortion of love, but the purity, the resonant cymatic frequency of love, is pure" said Ethan.

"You know what it is as well. I think we've been so busy with the patriarchal stuff that we've forgotten, or simply not realised, that women can be just as dangerous yet more deviant. I'm not just talking about the women of today, I mean the ancient feminine." I reply.

"And that's why I told you the Martians got so pissed off at the Lemurian culture because they let the place get hit," Ethan reflects back to another conversation we were having previously about early planetary colonisation and the politics that arose in those early years.

"I dunno about that honey, I dunno about the Lemurian story. I'm not sure about that timeline," I intuit.

"It's the cyclic nature of the women. See here's the thing, the women want to say they came first, but both men and women come first. We need to get to where the two become one. There's no matriarchy, there's no patriarchy, there's a holarchy instead. In a holarchy, we now have systems that come together as one. Where the energies are balanced as a singular unit. It's not a dichotomy; it's a unity," Ethan posits.

"My prayer is that I can continue to invoke this lost part of me that I forgot about, and remember it's there. And what it does for me is it... it's like... I don't really know how to explain it... It's like having nature on your side, by my side," I try to explain.

"That's right. And there is no side anymore, it's just 'one with'," said Ethan.

"As me, in me," Kate reconciled.

"And you as it, yes," said Ethan.

I nodded and felt a weight had lifted. I realised after discussing this whole experience with Ethan that we have understand our own unique story, on our own personal levels. Perhaps these memories or ways of perceiving reality is what my own subconscious mind needs to make sense of it all. Not to say that this story is made up, but that many stories are based on something real. The story is in in actual fact how we can navigate its territory and more fully understand it. Anything you can think of can be real and practical in some way. For me, I realised my journey would consist of trying to understand and accept the truth of what I had experienced so far. Different pieces of the puzzle would continue to unfold, I realised, and I would just have to keep following the signs and asking for clarity when I needed it. Which is precisely what I did when trying to understand what this whole situation was about. I prayed that this experience would somehow rewire me in a way that would make me stronger.

Next, we decided to go check out the second route to the right of the forest. As we followed the path along an already carved out trail, we were met with lots of muddy areas and tons of mosquitoes. After a while, I could tell that Ethan was becoming increasingly frustrated with the unknown surroundings, and I would have been too if it were not for the fact that I could feel the magic of this forest all around me. Somehow I knew the trees and the animals were watching us, and every time I would look into the sun-kissed canopy of leaves, I felt as though this moment was all that mattered. The harder the trail got, deep within this forest, the more I kept chanting to myself silently 'I trust in my path'. This mantra had come into my mind a few weeks prior, and I knew it was essential as I had even remembered to say it during some of my recent dreams. Especially ones that had taken an awkward turn. Within my thoughts, I had somehow remembered to say 'I trust in my path' and this simple mantra had helped me to overcome obstacles within the dream. Now, as I said this mantra in the forest, I felt as though something was waiting for us at the end of this path, and I could not keep from smiling the whole way.

As we finally came to a clearing and a bridge after about thirty minutes of walking through this magnificent forest, I saw what I thought looked to be a map, in a frame attached to a tree. I pointed out the structure to Ethan, and as we crossed the bridge, I began to realise that this frame was something else. As I stood in front of the picture, I could hardly believe what I was seeing. It was black and white sketching of a cat in a woman's arms. I gasped as I turned to Ethan and laughed at the astonishing synchronicity of finding this cat picture in this forest. I felt so incredibly grateful to the universe for giving me this sign of synchronicity. I then realised that this whole day had been a rite of passage. Seeing this cat picture at the end of our adventure made me realise that the previous healing I had done, and the remembrance of my cat self, was truly being gifted back to me in a most miraculous way. I took several pictures of this cat image and continued to smile the whole way home.

We were not entirely out of the forest, and as Ethan began talking about something or nothing, in particular, I had a deep, joyful feeling within my being. I basked in this inner conversation going on with my feeling body. Suddenly, we began to hear the voices of adults and children playing. The forest had led us to the back gardens of peoples large houses. Though, we were able to pass through the woods unnoticed. The whole time we viewed these gigantic houses and heard several families playing together in their pools, celebrating this Canadian holiday. I realised instantly that this was to be our own dream of our future together. I recognised now that the universe was showing us this—great big houses next to the forest, with families, laughing and playing together—to show us that what we desired was more than possible, it was on the way to us very soon.

This whole experience, I concluded was one that would help me realise my spirit animal was finally back with me—as the cat picture in the forest had demonstrated to me. After releasing the witches curse, I felt as though deep DNA healing and activation had taken place within me. I was healing this not only for myself but for my ancestors and the morphogenic field of the generations to come. I began to truly own my cat self and had rewired my body to go straight to courage instead of the fear-body. Several days after this event occurred, I began to notice how my body seemed even more sensitive as I could sense into energy more readily. In moments of anticipation or fear, I had a habit of going into my panic body. And on some of the worst days even fainting from the overwhelm.

Now though, after this experience, I began to channel and ground the energy through my whole body properly. My hands felt extremely powerful when I did this. Almost as though I was consciously transforming this negative energy into healing energy and sending it all to my hands. Instead of retracting into myself when I noticed my energy scattering, I directed the heat above and below my body. This helped to ground and elevate me at the same time. It made me feel more alive and aware than ever before. I could feel my body vibrating with energy and excitement when I conscouisly directed my energy along with my intuitive voice guiding me.

A RITE OF PASSAGE

TWELVE

Dream Work

∞

OVER THE FOLLOWING weeks, time seemed to slow down again. Ethan and I both began to feel a lull in the spirit in our lives. We were spending too much time with our worries. Instead, we decided to work with—and be grateful for—what we already had in our lives. Since we both work from home, we chose to clean and clear our space. After watching a Feng Shui expert during an online class, both of us were inspired to apply the principles to our home. We were determined to clear out anything that we did not need so that our space could feel more sacred. Changing our space around did wonders for our sense of energy flow and made us even more grateful for what we already had. Applying some of the Feng Shui principles we had learnt, we were able to see our rooms and the four directions in a whole new way. We had a dedicated altar to every single direction, which helped to remind us of our main goals in life.

Every day felt like a struggle, but we knew we had to be patient and continue to dream big whilst taking action towards our goals. We maintained our spiritual studies on the daily and began to work together more often. We were both inspired by learning about Celtic and Shamanic wisdom. Through these studies, I had come across the importance of our dreams—not just the ones we had during the day, but more so, the ones we had at nighttime. I had always felt extremely interested in the metaphors that my dreams so often presented. Only now, in my adulthood, did I sometimes recognise a divine hand intricately designing these so-called dreams. These dreams seemed more like a movie that had been handcrafted just for my consciousness. I had to start remembering their messages more often, I thought, especially if I wanted to lucid dream.

I was more inspired than ever to start recording my dreams as often as possible. Some of them continued to elude me even in writing them down. However, I began to notice that I recalled more dreams every night. I had also become lucid in a few of them. This was exciting, and even though the progress seemed slow, I started to believe in 'dreaming consciously' you would 'die consciously' which ultimately meant living consciously. Connecting with my dreams, and trying to decode their messages, instilled a type of power in me that enabled bridging the gap between both spiritual and material worlds. The Feng Shui clearing of our space had facilitated this even more so it seemed.

Dream Journal

21st of June, Summer Solstice...

I went to a type of museum by myself. Inside was very dark, and I was the only person in the room, which had an Egyptian tomb. Walked up to the grave and go to take a look inside. Suddenly, I am met with some girls from my high school who come over and start talking to me and the group. I remember the feeling of not really wanting to share my energy with them as we gathered round in a circle together. All of a sudden, one of the girls faint, and they all leave the room. Once they have left the room, I notice a letter that had dropped from the ceiling onto the ground detailing that 'I was not permitted entry' anymore. I open the Egyptian tomb hatchet anyway, but there is nothing inside. Feeling determined to find more, I see a door and a ladder that leads to a dark cellar. I begin to descend the steps, and my bare feet climb further and further down the ladder. As I do, I am met with electric twinges of pain in my feet, which I recognise to be vertigo. I realise that I am too afraid to continue descending these ladders alone in the dark and so I begin to climb back up the ladder.

Now that I am afraid suddenly, I tell myself in the dream 'I trust in my path'. At the same time, I try to see if there is a light switch in this place. I spot the light switch, and as I go to reach for it, I look down and realise how close I came to falling just now. Another electric twinge of pain covers my body now, and before I can press the light switch, I wake up feeling somewhat afraid.

After this dream, I realised the ladder into the basement represented going down into the depth of my unconscious. I later found out that this was not advised in the dream world. Instead, it was recommended to ask the dream to show me on the main level whatever it wished for me to see.

25th of June...

Had many dreams tonight about the sun and the moon. Woke up in between dream states praying to these celestials and feeling a deep loving connection to them in my being. In one of the dreams this night I stumble upon someone's backyard and decide it is the perfect place to camp my tent. Just as I am drawing a circle around my tent, I realise this is not the first time I have been to this garden. As I am finishing the last part of the ring, someone comes out to smoke, and when I ask them directly if it is ok for me to camp here, they tell me yes, no problem. So I start chatting with this person a little out of courtesy for letting my stay there. Though, I had the sense that I was meant to focus on something else instead. The dream ended before I could have a chance to figure out what I was doing there.

Woke up from this dream feeling a sense of joy after downloading a thought, telling me to notice synchronicity in everyday life. Understanding how profound it is to see how the mini and macro things in life consciously communicating and connected. These synchronicities in daily life are always happening according to divine timing. Which ultimately means everything is perfect as it is but continues to grow and expand everyday! I realise that I am to take the opportunity to always look for these beautiful possibilities in life. Even within the mundaneness of everyday living, there is magic in the darkness. Divine synchronicity lives there too. In abundance, in fact. This morning was a change to my usual experience of waking up feeling low and weirded out by my dreams.

27th of June...
Had a dream that involved making friends with an enemy I had from school. The next part of the vision was a carry on from the previous one but with different people and surroundings. All of a sudden there was this loud, abrasive noise coming from an orb on the TV, but the sound was all around us in the dream too. The sound was so abrasive and obtrusive. I managed to record the last five seconds of it on my phone in the dream. Then I tried to show this to my family to warn them what was going on with the outside world, but they did not believe me. The next moment I am sat in a classroom from school, with a teacher I have never seen before, but I immediately feel a resonance with her energy. I tell my ex-enemy who happens to be sat next to me, what had happened with the deafening orb and she seems to believed me. We conclude it must be some kind of directed-sound-brain controlling device that is being used to try and cause

mass telepathic control of people.

Suddenly, the teacher, who was smiling, is now frowning as she walks towards a door leading off from the classroom. I follow her into what looks to be a Greek-style looking bathroom, and she begins pumping the water faucet furiously. Her face is now against the bathroom wall, and she is crying out for someone to come back, some kind of goddess associated with the water. The water starts to overload the sink and the orbic interference happens again. People are suddenly panicking since no one knows what it is, but they can hear it piercing their eardrums. This orb looked to be colourful but synthetically made, and I woke up from a dream feeling scared and disconcerted.

This dream reminded me of the importance of honouring water. We use it all day long and rarely do we remember to thank it or set an intention with it. Many studies have shown, water reacts to your thoughts throughout the day. Today I will intend: I appreciate the water that I drink and wash with. Thank you for cleansing and healing my body.

28th of June...

Both Ethan and I are in the dream together, on separate snowmobiles. We are in a freezing country with lots of snow, though I sense this place is from some time in the future. We are there to gather plants that have survived through the snow and collect samples of each. Suddenly, we are talking to a family who seems very friendly to us, and we invite them back to our house to eat some vegetables.

1st of July...

I remember sitting on an old couch with Ethan, and as I looked into his eyes, all of a sudden, he had sunglasses on, something he never wears. As I look into the sunglasses, I see a man in the reflection—as me(!)—and freak out in the dream. All of a sudden, I can hear an echo in my voice, which feels very strange. Next, Ethan's mum comes into the room and begins talking about furniture as she watches a man out the window claiming for himself a couch that was left outside for the garbage men to pick up. Then, Ethan mentions that there is someone upstairs, and my attention immediately goes to our attic living space, and I wake up feeling as though there is someone in the room.

2nd of July...
In the dream, I am taking care of one of my young students who has come to visit me in England. I am also with an old friend, and we begin walking through a forest, which I sense is a shortcut home. Suddenly we are in front of a dark place that has a big pool of water. Having to get from one side to the other, a single tree trunk forms a bridge across the stream. Then we realise there is a queue of people waiting to get across this bridge, so we end up having to wait for what feels like an eternity in the dream. I give my students a piggyback and try to walk calmly across this tree log when I spot a colossal whale jumping out of the water. The dream ends with me saying, 'I trust in my path.'

3rd of July...
After watching a film called Mary Magdalene last night, I had a dream where I saw the real-life of Jesus, through his own eyes. I saw that Jesus had to deal with a lot of guilt for people dying for him.
Later, the dream shifts to more of the same school dream where I am continually searching for my classes and worrying that I will fail my exams.

After discussing this frequent dream with Ethan, I realise that going back to school and worrying about missing my classes all the time, is directly related to my own life presently. Technically, we are all in the 'school of life' right now, and concerned about where we are meant to go next in society. So concerned, that I forget to listen to my inner voice. Ethan suggests that next time I have another dream at school, instead of worrying, go to the class that I feel like going to the most. That way I don't let my timetables define where I should be in life but my heart.

8th of July...
Had a pleasant dream involving being at a large house with lots of people. I felt accomplished at one point in the dream having found everything that I needed there. The best part of the experience was having a conversation with the owner of this house who told me I had to keep on dreaming big if I wanted my dreams to come true. Not just with secret gardens, but with ideas like going to the moon.

Later on in the dream, a distant family relative called me up and told me how proud of me she was and that we could use her land for our permaculture business.

This was the complete opposite of a dream I had recently, where a family member was telling me how much everyone hated me? Bizarre.

10th of June...
Met with some African women. One of them tried to give me the number of someone wanting to tutor with me. But every time I went to write down the name, it did not work. Next, I was transported to my old home in England, where I grew up. I found a girl living there who left as soon as I showed up. Standing in the kitchen, I looked out the front window to see a huge lion trying to get in the house. Eventually, this lion did get into the house, so I ran out into the front garden, but the lion followed me. I quickly went to my knees tand tried to think positive thoughts, and the lion came over and licked my hands instead.

I felt grateful for this interaction with my spirit animal and proceeded to speak to her through light language the next morning. Was able to connect with that beautiful place that feels like home again.

15th of June...
Dreamt of playing an online game that filled my time growing up called World of Warcraft. I felt guilty playing this game as I was also supposed to be teaching at the same time. Instead, I went to a beautiful zone within the game with some elvish music playing in the background. All of a sudden, I was a character in the game. I proceeded to fall down a massive drop with my horse, and was now dead and had to be resurrected. Then a man in a boat came across the water to resuscitate me, and I woke up feeling a mix of emotions.

31st of July...
I was able to breathe through and be more aware of my dreams last night, was really cool. I felt like I was more in control of them and was less involved in the dramas that would take place. As though I was developing my mind and heart qualities together, to keep balance within my system. With my eyes shut, in between dreams, I kept feeling the urge to want to roll them from side to side. As I did I honoured the four corners of the world, North, East, South and West with my eyes darting to each corner. The whole experience felt like I was able to be more aware of myself in the dream state, a little bit like lucid dreaming but different. I was able to feel and sense into where my thoughts and dreams were operating from throughout the night.

5th of August...
This night's dream involved being back at my old house getting ready for school, with the same usual angst. Then the situation morphed into another place, and I saw myself as another woman. She was very wise, and it felt good to meld with her somehow.

DREAM WORK

Have a full month off from writing down my dreams to take in what I have learned so far. I begin looking into dream symbolism and try to make sense of some of the more essential metaphors that repeat within my dreams.

Then, around the 23rd of September, I was reintroduced to this idea from spirit. I hear a voice telling me to abstain from plant medicine for the next few weeks and start recounting my dreams again.

THE CHRONICLES OF SYNCHRONICITY

THIRTEEN

A Sun Dance Birthday

∞

As THE DAYS progressed, we both began to further understand our powers as Empaths. We continued our in-depth studies of spirituality and began to understand the skills and talents that sensitive people could possess. My Energy Alchemy course had now almost come to completion. It was coming up to my twenty-fifth birthday right around the same time, and we had planned to venture to a nearby nature reserve and stay in an Airbnb for the weekend. We figured we would post the finished course on the date of my birthday, The Lion's gate. This way, we could finally relax after months of hard work. Even more exciting was the prospect of spending time in the mountains and ancient forests of this sacred land together.

Though the course had been a stressful endeavour, including setbacks technologically, we had overcome them each time. I felt some relief at finally finishing these long weeks of hard work, though I still struggled to fully rest and not work. By the following week, we felt so tired and ready to take a break from it all. It was time to enjoy some well-needed rest in the quietness and solitude of nature.

We chose a serenely beautiful spot next door to a lake, which had its own beach. Looking at pictures of the whole place gave me fairy vibes. I could not wait to get there and hear the beautiful sounds of nature. A well-needed break from the constant hum of cars, trains, and construction workers at home. We spent the whole car trip blasting out old tunes, snacking on nuts, and freshly squeezed orange juice. I was excited about our new adventure.

By the time we arrived in Algonquin, I had noticed a profound shift in the quality of air of this place. My head tension also seemed to subside as we were fully surrounded by lush greenery. Gargantuan rocks, tall trees, and clear lakes reflected the azure blue sky above for the remainder of the car ride. We finally pulled up at the driveway of our hosts, and they greeted us warmly. Our place looked even better than the photos. It had taken us almost four hours to get there, and as we stood looking at the glistening lake right in front of our living room window, I felt as though even a ten-hour trip here would also have been worth it.

The first few days turned out to be more chill and relaxed than I had anticipated. It had rained for the first few days, and I had taken frequent naps during the early afternoons, something I never usually did. I felt so relaxed at the tranquillity of this place and so it provided some good rest. These frequent naps to rejuvenate myself became enjoyable. At the same time as taking naps, I continually found myself crying a lot during the day as I was still dealing with some emotional wounds that I had not yet adequately dealt with. I noticed how the universe kept sending people into my world, mainly digitally, that continuously triggered my old patterns and beliefs of not being good enough. I had some deep wounds yet still to heal. Though with Ethan by my side, I realised that just me, him and nature was all I truly needed to feel at peace.

Once the sunshine came, we made several hiking trips through the nature reserve trails. The views were spectacular and were food for my soul. During our walks, we could often sense into the presence of animals watching, too, which felt homely. The air was so incredibly clean and fresh as we wandered deep within the ancient forests all around. It had been such a relaxingly splendid holiday that when our last day rolled around, I felt a deep urge to want to stay. I felt as though I could live in this place forever. I got to experience the sacred nature of this place that had been cared for by the community. This area of Canada had been protected and preserved, unlike many other towns. Here Gaia was allowed to grow into productive ecosystems. There was twice as much life here than anywhere in the city.

On our last day, we packed up our things and headed to the beach. It was only two minutes away from our cosy caravan. While there, I had an instinct to sing to the great goddess of the lake. Channeling some harmonic tones to thank the goddess of the water for her great spirit of protection over this heavenly place. Later, some people joined us on the beach. We sat relaxing in the sun, reading our books, as a man was leaving the beach, Ethan turned to ask where the Powwow was. He had overheard the man talking about it in conversation. He told us it was just down the road and if we went quickly, we could catch the beginning of the ceremony.

After speedily buying our tickets, we drove down a long winding road into the forest, and arrived just in time for the grand opening ceremony. We purchased our wristbands, and an overwhelming sense of awe came over me as I felt that we were exactly where we needed to be. What a stroke of luck or rather, synchronicity, to now be at a Powwow, I thought. I had always wanted to experience a Powwow in real life, and now here we were, a place that we didn't know existed just several minutes ago. We had made it just on time, as lots of smiling faces were in the space. I laughed at the divine synchronicity of it all and knew we were going to have a brilliant last day on holiday.

As we walked into where the ceremony was being hosted out in nature, I noticed the fantastic scenery all around us. We were in the middle of a vast forest clearing, right next to a tranquil lake that sat beside a high mountain. The Native people had undoubtedly chosen this sacred place to perform their ceremony for a reason. Along the edges of the clearing were little stalls selling lots of different Native American trinkets, and I had wished to buy them all, but unfortunately, we did not think to bring the cash.

Having always adored the native jewellery, beaded bracelets, necklaces and earrings, I asked Ethan if we could find a place to draw out some money. I wanted to buy something as a reminder of our experiences in this sacred land. I had my heart set on some earrings, but Ethan told me that I should wait instead, as something this sacred should be gifted to me. I nodded, not knowing how that would happen, and we walked into the area where many people had gathered under a tipi. The drums had already begun, and we found a little spot on a bench that was free and began taking off our shoes and socks, placing our bare feet onto the earth. My feet instantly began tapping to the sound of the drums, and I could feel the momentum of the place building in grounded energy.

Just then, I noticed that Ethan appeared to be experiencing an emotional release and some clearing of his own. He had tears rolling down his cheeks and was clearly dealing with something. I asked if he was okay for reassurance, and he told me he was releasing his fears and felt safe to do so in this space. Ethan's emotional release made sense to me, as we were still dealing with the constant unknown as to what exactly we were here to do in this life.

Due to a miscommunication at my workplace regarding the timing of my resignation, my teaching contract had ended a few weeks early, just weeks before my year anniversary with them. Though, I took this as a sign that I was supposed to find something else that resonated with me instead. Ethan too was not sure when his next job would arise. Instead of worrying about our money concerns, we decided to embrace the emotional healing and take part in the celebrations that were happening right before our eyes.

We gladly watched several different styles of native dance. Each one of them lit up my heart with a deep love for these people. I couldn't help losing my self in the feeling that I had been part of this style of celebration before—although not in this lifetime, for sure. As we enjoyed the entertainment, an old native man came to have a chat with us and commented on the synergy between us both. I felt grateful for this interaction, and we realised that we now felt ready to join in the celebrations ourselves. First, though, we decided to take a quick hike in the forest and smoke some cannabis. At first, I did not like the idea. I did not want to offend anyone with what would be perceived as a 'drug' to some. But I knew, deep in my heart, that this sacred plant was often misrepresented. It was a medicine that on the right occasion, in moderation, could help to elevate one's spirit into even more joy and love.

I realised during my time with the plant, using sacred prayer and intention before vaping cannabis was a great way to show gratitude and respect. We both set the intention to co-create with cannabis to connect more fully in the present moment, with the love of community, and the love of mother earth. As we sat in the forest, we heard what sounded to be a wolf's call. Several times we listened to this howl, and although a part of me was afraid that we might be in danger, another part of me felt into the divine connection of it all. It seemed that the wolf was howling in synch with the drums, which reminded me of how close these types of celebrations were to nature's own heart. Once we finished the pipe, we walked back to where the Powwow was taking place. Two beautiful, young girls began walking towards us that I had previously seen on the way in. There was something so innocent and loving in one of the girl's eyes that I could not quite put my finger on. She looked at me and asked if my bohemian pants were a skirt, I shook my head, and she laughed, telling me how cool she thought they were.

I took note of how moments of profound feeling observation, like this, would always have a way with my heart. Perhaps the resonant energy I previously noticed in these girls was then later reciprocated in some way. We walked into the main gathering area, where there stood a quaint hut for all the dancers and drummers. Mesmerised by the beautifully intricate and colourful outfits these Natives adorned, I almost missed the call to join the All Nations Dance. When I realised this meant that everyone could join the Sun Dance, I scooped up the opportunity to celebrate in a heartbeat. I could not wait to experience the grounding and free-flowing dance that came with this fantastic community of young and old.

Although my clothes were not as stunning as the native's regalia, I happened to be wearing white and blue which I happened to feel good in. Incredibly, the native's had diligently made their regalia a whole year before the ceremony. Each and everyone had an attractive array of all the colours from the rainbow. Gorgeous patterns, feather decorations, as well as little bells that made music to scare away the evil spirits when they danced in this adorned clothing. One girl who was dancing in front of me had colourful wings that floated in the wind. I saw her as a butterfly dancing around the circle the whole time. Ethan and I, of course, stuck out like a sore thumb since there were not many 'westerners' there. But for some reason, Ethan had decided to wear white that day, too. With the beat of the drum becoming more powerful, I grounded into my feet, as though I was sensing deeper into mother earth. I began to imagine golden roots that attached to my soles and connected with the land fully as I danced around on the solid ground.

When the drumming stopped, I heard an announcement that there would apparently be a winner of a prize for the best dance. I automatically sensed who the winner would be, as I had watched her float around the circle most of the dance. The butterfly girl did indeed win, and she seemed happy about it. Once the next dance had started, we went and found a quiet spot nearby the lake in which we could still view the central area. We sat there eating some cherries and intently planting the seeds in the ground. I felt the need to listen intently to these people, as many tribe's men and women told their story over the microphone.

After feeling full from all the cherries we had eaten, I heard an announcement of a warm-hearted lady call out, "Okay, it's another All Nations Dance again! And this time, if you win, you will get a pair of beaded earrings."

I looked at Ethan and knew that this was my chance. I tried not to overthink about winning the earrings, although I sincerely wanted to. Instead, I smiled at the synchronicity and released any attachment to receiving such a gift. I quickly scooted over to the central circle, and the whole time, I danced and grounded into the earth. I felt my energy body connected with the many other people that danced around too. While dancing, I looked to the sky and could not keep the smile off my face. I was expressing my gratitude to Father universe and laughed heartily for the majority of the dance because I felt 'home'.

So at peace, seamlessly in the flow with everything there, I danced around the ring and felt ancestors there with me. When the drumming finally stopped, I had almost completely forgotten about the earrings. All of a sudden, I was given some gorgeous, black, white, red and yellow shell earrings. Overwhelmed with joy, the man was gone before I could thank him. I put my hands together in a prayer motion and bowed my head to the audience. Next, I saw a lady with a microphone rushing over to me, and she spoke into the microphone.

"What's your name?"

"Kate," I smiled and nodded.

"That's my name too!" she said excitedly.

I felt joyful by this notion and had a burst of gratitude wash over me as I hugged her.

"Where are you from?" she asked.

"We live just outside of Toronto, but I am originally from England." My voice quivered a little as I realised now that everyone was watching me.

"All right, well, thank you for joining us here today, Kate," she said as she walked away.

I had desperately wanted to tell each and every person there how grateful I was for this ceremony, but my nerves got the better of me. Instead, I held the love and gratitude in my heart as I put the earrings on, and walked back to our little corner by the lake.

"Well, there you go, I told you the earrings had to be a gift," Ethan said smugly.

"You were right" I replied.

My senses seemed merrily present to all that was going on within this place. The tribe had politely asked that no one take any pictures or video. This removed the urge for me to want to capture these precious moments on film and instead, I captured these sacred moments within my soul. I saw one of the chief elders approaching us, who I had noticed as soon as we first arrived. His smile spoke of a warm heart and a kind soul in more ways than words ever could. I could not keep the smile off my own face as he approached us.

"Do you have a phone?" he asked us both.

Ethan handed his phone to the elder. He smiled and told us he was going to take a picture of us as the scenery behind looked perfect.

"What's your name?" I addressed the elder.

He reached out a hand, and I held it with both of mine as we shook hands. "Kevin," he replied.

Before I could tell him that this had been my grandfather's name, he asked me the same question. "Kate," I smiled.

"Ahh, yes, just like my sister!" he recounts.

"That's right. So do you guys come here every year?" I asked.

"Every year. Today is our 25th annual celebration," Kevin reflects with pride.

It dawned on me again how synchronistic this whole day had been. The earrings, the native elders... and now I realised, this 25th ceremony, which happened only once a year—on our last day here, just two days after my own twenty-fifth birthday. Wonderous synchronicity!

As if to give us one last gift, Kevin shared, "before the ceremony, we meditate from that mountaintop," and he pointed to the mountains behind us.

"That's amazing! Thank you," I said as he turned and began walking back toward the circle.

Just then a great-grandma of the tribe began her speech. Her words were so full of wisdom, love and honour that the declaration made me cry. I felt like I knew that old grandma somehow, she was not old at all really, she was wise and carried youthful energy about her. She was the divine feminine that I felt was missing in the world today. She had a harmonic balance of masculine and feminine power about her. After this beautiful speech, we realised it was getting late and bid farewell to everyone. We still had a long journey ahead of us to make it home. Every cell of my being did not want to leave this place. It felt like home, and I wanted to stay with these people and celebrations. But I knew we would have a fun time describng the synchronicities to each other on the ride home.

I recollected the days events and realized I had felt free to be fully empowered in my own energy, yet connect openly and lovingly with the community. This new sense of freedom and joy had manifested a perfect day for us. I wondered why every day could not be like this. Ethan too had felt the sacredness of what had taken place for us this day. Being a part of this venerable Powwow had connected us deeply to our native roots. It had also instilled a newfound commitment to honour and celebrate Mother Nature's beauty. Ethan had been able to clear his fears and felt much more grounded after the whole experience. I thought about the deep connection I had experienced with these people all the way home. My heart ached somewhat at the thought of never seeing this kind of community again. Though, I knew, we would be back.

A SUN DANCE BIRTHDAY

THE CHRONICLES OF SYNCHRONICITY

FOURTEEN

Space of Love

∞

THE FIRST SIGNS of autumn were upon us with the shifting of humid air into cold, crisp fall breezes. The leaves had now started to turn golden and crunched beneath our feet every morning. Nature was now getting ready for the dark nights, which followed the bright light of the summertime. A great sense of stillness began to arise within me. I started to sense that my time for going inward, into the silence of the void, had arrived. I thought about how many ascended masters, such as Jesus and Buddha, took this path. When they dropped off the face of the Earth for extended periods and came back reborn and ready to share their message.

I recognized a call from within that my soul was now beckoning me to take time for rest and go much more slowly within my everyday life. Simple tasks began to turn into a form of meditation, such as doing the washing up and vacuuming. I felt the need for conversation much less and continued to welcome the moments of complete silence within my mind. My thoughts occasionally just disappeared, entirely out of sight.

Everything was beginning to fall into place as Ethan, and I

continuously followed the signs and synchronicities that arose. Most of which were messages from spirit that led us to develop specific strings of thoughts and feelings. This helped us to choose gratitude instead of worry. We had made a conscious decision to put our spiritual development and love before anything else. We knew that this inward development would be the basis for all of our other avenues to come about. Including the material abundance, we so longed for. Both of us were beginning to understand each other from the perspective of being one single unit. Even tapping into each other's thoughts and ideas without having a verbal conversation.

One night as we both laid in bed, while Ethan was fast asleep, another vision began to form in my mind. An image of our cosy house in the woods came to me again. This comfortable cabin vision had started many years ago when I used to fantasize that I lived in a forest as a young girl. After my days spent adventuring the wild in this vision, I would return home to my intimate cabin and feel a warm sensation of comfort. Here in this cabin, my family members would greet me heartily. Everyone was enjoying each other's company together. As I climbed the stairs and went toward my bedroom, it was a quaint space that housed several other sleeping sisters and brothers. Every time I would climb into my bed, feeling an immense amount of peace and comfort there. I felt safe being surrounded by so many members of the family. There was something so tranquil about the fresh smells and sounds of nature right outside our window. As well as the golden light that surrounded the many happy faces of laughter inside this cabin.

On this particularly chilly Autumnal evening, I had this same vision, yet it was ever so slightly different. Instead of being one of the children coming home to go to sleep, I saw myself as a nurturing mother figure instead. I was no longer one of the children tucked up all cozy in the bed with the rest of the children. This time I embodied the motherly role as I joyfully roamed throughout the comfortable cabin. Humming a sweet song of peace as I turned out the golden lamps throughout the house. I saw myself going towards the bedroom and tucking all of the children into bed. I felt deep strength and pure satisfaction throughout my energy body.

Sitting with the images and feelings that came with this vision for a while, I realized it was trying to show me some of my most profound dreams and desires. The vision was helping me to recognize that my actual goals in this lifetime were to nurture children and animals. Most of my joy was spent teaching, learning and growing alongside them. For the remainder of the evening, I began to feel the pangs of maternal instinct kicking in as I so longed for a child of our own someday.

The next morning I stepped outside with even more gleefully than usual, I loved to spend my days singing to the rabbits, squirrels, birds and chipmunks. I cheerfully noticed how they seemed to be communicating with me, through the language of feeling somehow. Birds and chipmunks came closer and closer everyday, sometimes landing or crawling on my head and hands. The squirrels would occasionally fall asleep to my singing. Some days they would be eating their apples with what seemed like a joyful expression on their little faces. Often the chipmunks would surprise me with tiny movements, winking and even moving their arms to the sound of my voice. Bunny rabbits began to relax and let loose around us both too. Kicking and flapping their little feet and tails around the garden as they would play together. We counted more baby bunnies by the weeks, each of whom were brave enough to say hello, telepathically revealing their names to me. Chickadees came to my handful of food and moved their beak as though speaking with me. I longed to have an even deeper connection with them. To know precisely what they felt and thought about life and their home in our secret garden. Time spent with these animals and elementals were some of the most precious moments in my life.

Ethan and I both sensed the importance of the role we were both playing within our secret garden. We worked with the notion of opening to the elemental wisdom on the daily. Designing and saving up for our new garden and dream home together. We knew that we could not stay where we were forever since we wanted children. We printed off images of the house of our dreams and placed them all over the walls in the attic, every once in a while. Fully determined to work hard to make our dreams come to life. Our future dream looked similar to the cosy cabin in the woods—but with a body of water around the edges of the secret garden's perimeter. There would be catchment systems, which housed many different arrays of water, for drinking, swimming and flowing fountains. It would have sacred spaces for wishing wells and spiritual mazes. Trees to pray and set intentions with, as well as yoga and tent areas for music and dance.

This first training ground, our current secret garden, was a place of love. The wise and beautiful trees within our backyard began to whisper words of wisdom to me daily. I would often feel the urge to channel their poetry and write it down. They would ask me to be quiet and listen to what the air whistled, to what the sea sang, and what the Earth felt. They told me to dance with the stars and shine my light as often as possible. To always choose this moment right now, as well as allow for all that ever would be. This wisdom came from many different types of trees in the garden. We had several of them—but five of them, in particular, stood out to me. Especially the apple tree, which I frequently sat under to write. Our apple tree gave the gift of beauty and creativity. I would find myself to be more creative while sitting underneath it. Coming into our garden both morning and evening, to relax and enjoy watching Nature's TV.

Our secret garden was not just a way for us to escape the

density of the modern world. It was a place that we came to feel fully connected to Mother Nature and ourselves. A place we could connect to our own body, mind and soul, through the nurturing love of great Gaia. Our secret garden, of the present and the future, enlivened our senses. The warm breeze that caressed our skin. The sweet aromas that tickled our noses. Even the relaxing orchestra of insects and animals all around us provided inspiration. It was a magical space, a place we had been dreaming of all our lives. A sacred sanctuary. There were a plethora of imperceivable living beings within this garden, including the Fairy Folk. Often we would wander into the garden and communicate with it in many different ways, sharing food and appreciation with it. Whether it was through words of gratitude or songs of beauty. We focused on our connections with Mother Earth and Father Universe as often as we could.

The birds, chipmunks, raccoons, rabbits and squirrels, were all family to us. I felt the purest expression of love around them, which would make me giddy like a child again. When the days were not so bright, and confusing emotions of fear would appear, our secret garden would teach us how to be patient. It encouraged us to listen and be aware of the whole spectrum of reality that was really taking place behind the veil. There was always something new to explore within our secret garden. It was ever-changing and expanding in the same way that we were. The alternating seasons created a new phenomenon for us to marvel at every day. From geometrically perfect snowflakes to dewy grass, there was always something changing to observe in Gaia's garden. The flowers, leaves, and trees grew more prominent and beautiful with each passing day. Our minds, too, began flourishing in creativity and abundance.

So many others, including friends and family, seemed to pass up the opportunity to be out in nature more often. This often baffled me, but I understood that to feel the essence of nature, you have to become still within. Maybe the excitement of cities and the hustle and bustle of everyday living seemed more practical to some. To us, the experience of being closer to nature herself was always profoundly more enjoyable. In Druidry, as well as other nature-based spiritualities, there is the concept of a Sacred Grove. A patch of land is chosen for this particular reason and is then considered sacred and of special importance. We can use these ancient old practices of creating a Sacred Grove or secret garden for ourselves in the present day.

While reading up on many different books and articles surrounding the notion of a secret garden, I came across some synchronistic quotes I'd like to share with you:

"And the secret garden bloomed and bloomed and every morning revealed new miracles." - **Frances Burnett**

"Prayer is like a secret garden made up of silence and rest and inwardness. But there are a thousand and one doors into this garden, and we all have to find our own." - **Jean Vanier.**

"Both abundance and lack exist simultaneously in our lives, as parallel realities. It is always our conscious choice which secret garden we will tend. When we choose not to focus on what is missing from our lives but are grateful for the abundance that's present. Love, health, family, friends, work, the joys of nature, and personal pursuits that bring us pleasure. The wasteland of illusion falls away, and we experience Heaven on earth." - **Sarah Ban Breathnach**

I regularly pondered how society so easily pulled us into the sways of addiction to consumerism. Some media especially lures us towards feelings of anger, mistrust, sadness, and less towards our own inner truth. What we realized after these many years seeking nature first, is that it taught us to be vigilant of what we put our attention and focus on. If we wanted to see changes happen in our lives, then we had to start being the change by focusing on what made us happy and peaceful. Somehow these secrets were often revealed to me by spending time in the garden. The secret door or gateway to my own secret garden was to be found internally.

It was our strong values that made sure that we were following our bliss as often as possible. Instead of following the crowd and what society told us was 'success' in life, we developed our own way from within. Humbling ourselves, we realized we already had everything we needed in terms of health, and quality of life. With this gratefulness, manifestation occurred in all sorts of unexpected ways. The idea of having children came up for consideration often. I was continually having conversations with our yet-to-be daughter during the days, somehow it seemed like she was already with us. With this secret garden and space of love, we were preparing a nurturing space for our children to be born into.

We concluded it was time to plan our wedding as a sacred ritual. One that would guide our readiness towards this union and promise to Life. Our true passions seemed to coincide together, which made it all the more magical, to have a shared vision for the future. We each were fascinated by learning how to bridge the gap between the magic of nature's physical reality, with the mystery of the metaphysical realms. Our garden would be our sacred ritual space to perform our very own wedding rite together. We set out to plan a small ceremony for the coming autumn equinox.

Three weeks before the wedding date, I had the instinct to start a nightly ritual along with Ethan. The ideas involved abstaining from any plant medicines (mainly cannabis) for several weeks, and instead, use this time to experience a type of meditation before sleep. This ritual would prepare us for the dream world to come, and maybe even potentially allow us to tap into our own awareness during sleep and lucid dreams. Here are the dreams I remembered during this time:

23rd of September...
I looked after a young girl who was not mine, but she felt like a daughter to me. Was driving around to places and trying to help her with things. I was predominantly playing a nurturing role in this dream.

I had been guided to set an intention this night and asked for a dream to clarify my connection to the feminine. Perhaps this suggests that my connection to the divine feminine is through a nurturing role? From this, I am aware of the fact that I am to nurture my own self, too, since this young girl could have represented me in the dream. I have always felt like I resonated with playing a nurturing role for others also.

25th of September...
Was back at my brother's place in England and now had a baby in my arms. It felt like this was my baby, although it did not look like me. I still felt so much love for how cute she was. Then I tried to find some privacy within the dream to breastfeed this little babe. In the dream, I was only able to breastfeed out of one breast, but I was incredibly happy about this as I felt grateful that I could breastfeed at all. It felt like a miracle, in fact.

26th of September...
I was in a far-off country somewhere, and the nature surrounding me was beautiful. All of a sudden, it turned to the nighttime, and there was a bar in front of me. I realised that I was there trying to help my dad's beer business that he had tried to set up years ago. As I was trying to help him though I kept having these negative spirits trying to attach to me and speak

through me. I could see them, and they kept trying to take over my thoughts and voice. I was trying to sleep next to my dad and was crying out for him to help me, but he was fast asleep. Woke up with my voice trembling.

Interesting that it was nighttime within this dream. Some dream interpretations suggest that nighttime in the dream reflects that which is being released and is no longer the truth of the matter. Sunrise or daylight in the dream represents that which is going to be manifested. This coincides well with the fact that in real life, my dad had no longer decided to create a beer business which I was quite happy about. The dream showed me that spirits who were alcoholics during their incarnations could attach to those who drink as a means of continuing their habit beyond death. These are usually souls that have unfinished business on earth or are still trapped in the material by obsessive habits. Since I used to drink alcohol frequently, this dream makes me realise how grateful I am to no longer partake in it.

30th of September...
Was with a native family at the beginning of the dream. Then I spent some time with everyone in the house. Eventually it came time to say goodbye and suddenly an old native woman, who I hadn't seen before, came up to me and gave me the most endearing hug. I could sense her energy so strongly as it was extremely calm and loving. Our hug was one of the most precious feelings, we hugged together for a long while. Her voice was so comforting to my ears.

Also dreamt about getting ready for school but not wanting to go. The whole time in the dream I am trying to tell myself to not go one minute and then the next minute telling myself that I will miss out if I don't go. Finally, I told myself I would not go. The next minute my brother is in my room. He is doing something there, and I ask him to get out as I don't appreciate his behaviour within the dream.

1st of October...
Went to a hostel, was sitting outside in a beautiful nature garden when suddenly I could hear some music. Decided to find out where it was coming from and followed the music to a maze looking building. It had many different levels, and as I traverse each one, entering different rooms, I feel called to greet everyone as I do. At one point, as I am nearing the end of this room maze, a big guy tries to stop me from leaving. I notice he has some disabilities and is much stronger than me, but I make it clear to him I won't stay. I scoot under his arms quickly, and on my way out of the building I step over a famous musician who rubs my foot and we both smile together.

Also had a dream later the same night in a vast meeting place of some sort. There were lots of people there, and I seemed to be dressed in and feel a sense of authority. I was meeting and greeting everyone, and before I could feel socially anxious, I corrected my thoughts and made sure to ask people, "how are you?" This made me feel more confident, and people seemed to respond well. We all seemed to be business people and decided to drive to different nature spots all of a sudden. We were looking for a place to put a statue which seemed necessary. We eventually drove back to my old home, and I told these people that there used to be nature fields in the back of our house. Now though, all we could see were houses everywhere.

2nd of October...
I walked to a restaurant with some people. We eventually had to crawl through a tiny space to get inside, we all felt very claustrophobic. Once inside, past the small entrance, the restaurant was huge, and two of my ex-friends from school shouted over to me. I nodded at them in response but carried

on to where I was going. I then sat at a table with my mum and brother. As I am trying to figure out what to eat my brother becomes annoyed, and before I know it, I am now in a mall trying to find something.

3rd of October...
Was with my other brother a lot in my dreams last night. He was driving me around and dropped me off at student halls that I was staying in. Before arriving there, I kept seeing ships in the sky, some were UFOs others were government ships. Everyone seemed to be very frantic within the area. The student halls were extremely dark and dingy, and I felt scared to stay there alone.

4th of October...
More dreams about school and not knowing my timetable. But felt better this time than any other dream at school before.

5th of October...
Ethan and I are travelling to different places, and I end up having an argument with his ex. Then I am transported to a pathway in a forest with a group of ladies. The older woman receives a message from the sky that is "not of grace" suddenly four animals begin chasing us. There was a bear, a wolf, a dog, and one other, which we are trying not to kill but run from.

Wake up to wonder if they were spirit animals or not?

6th of October...
Walking through the forests at home trying to get somewhere. Afraid to do what I needed to do in the fields as it is nighttime. I don't want to bring to much attention to myself, so I walk home instead. Now I'm at school but sitting in a classroom with two other friends, and we are taking it easy. Next, I am in a mall

wishing a friend farewell, and as I walk past lots of people in this mall, I get the sense that I am more 'aware' more than them within the dream. I feel light and smiley, while others look dark and sad.

7th of October...
Have to go somewhere with Ethan's stepdad who died earlier in the year. In the dream, I don't want to go anywhere with him but feel forced to get into the car. Ethan's stepdad is driving crazily, and I start to become fearful for my life when suddenly, I realise I am in a dream! Now that I am lucid, we are suddenly at our destination. I start singing at the top of my lungs to keep myself from being afraid. While the stepdad is away, I begin to imagine different instruments there with me in the car. This helps me to not feel the need to run away. Instead, I started to imagine a guitar, singing and playing it at the same time. Next, I think of a piano, and there it emerges. Finally, I think of a drum, and it appears before me. Playing these instruments feels really good and almost protective.

The next dream involves Ethan and me in our garden. The garden seems to be much larger in this place, and suddenly we notice these little creatures that look like native dwarves roaming through. I feel fascinated by these people and wish them well in the dream. I send them good wishes because I can sense they are very in-tune with nature and become fearful that the neighbours might try to kill them. We then go and sit in a different part of the yard, and all of a sudden a big dancing party of people comes by. Now we are sat inside of a building within the garden, and I notice someone from school there. I'm shocked to see her since this place seems very spiritual, and she had never taken an interest in such things. Then I notice other soft-spoken people from school there too, and we all start to join one another in a joyful dance party.

SPACE OF LOVE

THE CHRONICLES OF SYNCHRONICITY

FIFTEEN

The Wedding

∞

I HAD BEEN called to practise recalling my dreams for a long time. It just so happened that the days leading up to the wedding provided the push for us to get serious about it. These days before the wedding seemed essential, and I wanted my mind to be as clear as possible before the big day. Since childhood, I had always felt a pang of urgency every morning, knowing I had so many dreams that night, but not remembering much about them.

To do something about this, I created a 'dream week' schedule, that involved tasks for before, during, and after sleep. Before sleep, around six in the evening, we would begin the ritual with some gentle exercise or yoga, depending on how we felt. Once the blood was thoroughly pumping through our veins, we would then start to make some music. Depending on how we felt that day, with the guitar, our voice, or some drums. This would take us into a trance-like state where we relaxed more into our bodies and breath.

Next, we cleansed our sacred space, in front of our altar of dreams and success. We changed the layout of crystals on this altar every so often. Behind it, there were many pictures of our dream home and garden spaces. We would cleanse the area with natural sage and incense, holding an intention that it may cleanse and purify the air. Then we would proceed to use anointing oil that we made from essential oils and carrier oil. Again depending on how we felt, we would massage it into each other's shoulders or hands, and make a point of anointing our brows with it. Then we would get in a comfortable position and meditate or focus on breathing for at least fifteen minutes.

Once we had both come back around from meditation, we proceeded to use affirmations and mantras such as "I will lucid dream tonight." We would also continually ask ourselves "am I dreaming?" throughout the day, to habitually program our mind to become lucid. Establishing a plan once we were lucid in a dream involved choosing something to focus on. Such as asking for a dream of some kind that would help give answers to a burning question we had. If something was troubling us during our waking life, perhaps confusion about a specific situation, we could ask for a dream about it. One night I asked for an idea about 'understanding my social anxiety' to which I dreamt about a past life where something traumatic had happened to me during a social encounter.

Ethan and I discussed our shared intentions for dreams and hoped eventually, we would experience a shared vision in our secret garden together. Once we had decided on a meeting place within our dreams, we would close the ritual by giving a gratitude prayer towards our angels and ancestors and proceed to go to sleep. One night—after discussing the idea of our future selves being able to steward a whole new planet, a 'baby Earth', we both dreamt of a colourful world. Although we did not get to meet in the dream, the fact that we both had the same dream was fascinating to us.

During the dream state, another practise we had to remember was to stay calm and collected. Often during my past experiences with lucid dreaming, I would step outside and change the colours of the sky to pink and purple. I would get so excited by the notion that I would become overwhelmed in the dream. Therefore, our practice was to stay cool, calm, and collected during our lucidity. Once we were lucid, it was up to us to cast forth an image of our sacred space using our memory and visualisation, and then step into it. This required more training, as I noticed that it was challenging to keep up the momentum of controlling things in the dream. The skies would only stay pink and purple for as long as I focused on them doing so, as lucid dreaming required energy.

Through this practice, we came to realise that there seemed to be a personal film production company, spiritually making dream movies for us. Shamanic teachings had taught us that dreams were sometimes visitations from spirits. Potentially angels or even our future selves coming to give us messages or teach us sacred wisdom. We realised the more we tapped into our dreams, the more they would guide us in everyday life, even the gruesome ones carried a message. Shamanic teaching would go as far as to tell us to only act in the real world on the things we had dreamt about.

. . .

These two weeks flew by, and the big day finally arrived. It was an unusually warm autumnal day. We praised the Spirit of the Sun for gracing us since the whole wedding would be outdoors. Watching the sunrise and drinking our tea, I felt surprisingly relaxed and peaceful. The air was crisp and refreshing, and the heavenly breeze swept the leaves off the trees. The relaxing sounds of falling leaves sounded like little rain droplets from all around. We were more than ready for this day to unfold, even though we had only officially decided to get married two months before the ceremony. It took us only a short time to prepare due to the low-key nature of the planned wedding day. We had decided to only invite a small handful of the family that lived nearby. Planned on such short notice, the ceremony consisted of a small gathering of eleven. My family and friends from England were unable to join. Instead, we asked them to be there with us in spirit as it was going to be a special day of union between us both.

I quickly realised I wanted my family to witness this sacred day, even if they could not be present physically. So we decided to live stream the wedding to the rest of our family. Live streaming the wedding online meant that they could be part of the celebrations, too. We decided this wedding was going to be a sacred rite between both Ethan and me, and nature. We loved the idea of getting married in our secret garden, and the ability to share this with our family was exciting. We had prepared for our wedding day by designing a wedding rite and a whole ceremony to go along with it that was utterly unconventional and untraditional.

Ethan built us an arbour with wood, and we placed flowers, and some white flowing fabric on top for us to get married under. After this, everything had worked out synchronistically, mainly thanks to Ethan's mother. She had suggested that we go and look for the flowers to attach to the arbour, so we went to an art store. It seemed too expensive at first glance, but with a stroke of luck, before leaving the store, we walked straight past a massive flower sale. They were giving away bags of spring flowers for only four dollars. Once we got them home and counted all our purchases up, we realised they were worth at least two hundred dollars, and we had only paid sixteen. We took it as a good sign. These savings were very much appreciated and felt synchronistic. Ethan's mum had also suggested we get married by her old friend who happened to be a minister. She was sick on the day, but sent a replacement instead, who turned out to be an excellent option for us. With the original plans no longer in place, we chose to go with a Wiccan handfasting ceremony, as our new officiants' spiritual values aligned well with ours.

Inviting the family and proclaiming my true, authentic love for Ethan would be my most cherished experience yet. The idea behind this sacred union taking place was much more than declaring and bonding our passion together. We understood that the true essence of love is the feeling body of the universe, love connects us to the universal force of all that is. Thus the idea of a sacred marriage rite would inform our entire spirit that something far more significant was about to take place within this union. This marriage would be something that would benefit the larger body, beyond just us. It was also going to be the start of our new life together. We wrote our vows, shopped for our outfits, and even planned a visualisation throughout the whole ceremony together. We were going against traditional wedding 'rules', and it felt entirely right to do so.

After we had finished our tea, the morning of the wedding, I started to get ready. By two in the afternoon, my mother and sister-in-law had already made me look like a princess. With a white and purple flower crown and bohemian-style white dress. We then went to a favourite nature spot nearby with the family to take some wedding pictures. Once finished, we arrived home to start the celebrations immediately. We had set up several areas for people to sit, eat and relax while watching the ceremony. More so, we had given lots of gifts to our secret garden area, as a token of our appreciation of the elemental spirits and fair folk. We had made sure to let the animals know they were to join in on our celebrations, too. Throughout the day, we placed fruit and nuts out for all of the animals to come and enjoy. We wanted it to be everyone's special day, including Natures.

As everyone began to take their places, I set up my phone's camera to live stream the event to the rest of my family. Once live, I welcomed everyone who could not be there in person. Most of our family were not quite the same as us in loving nature so much, but they appreciated our garden space. I decided to explain to everyone why we were getting married in a garden, and why we let this garden grow wild. The common practice everyone seemed to do across the area involved mowing their grass weekly. Ethan and I, on the other hand, had decided to let our garden grow freely. It looked wild to some people, but to us, it was not just aesthetically pleasing but served a function too. It attracted all kinds of critters and was good for the birds, bees, flowers, and trees. Letting our garden grow wild even encouraged some creatures that were on the brink of extinction to stop by and say hello. We were living in a time of pesticides and chemicals, and the idea that gardens were measured by how they looked and not by what functions they served seemed absurd. I wanted to make it clear to my family why it was so important to let nature grow as it had brought so much magic into our world.

Time seemed to slow down, as it was only moments until I would walk down the aisle. I could feel my heart beating faster than ever, though I had a strongly odd sense of equanimity. I felt like a true nature princess as I stepped out barefoot to the sound of the harp playing. I walked up the aisle towards the wedding arch and felt the grand communion of it all. We stood underneath the arbour together. Ethan and I had a permanent smile on both of our faces, despite getting some of the vows wrong. I had chosen to read a promise from a series of books called 'Anastasia' that Ethan had gifted me with two Christmases ago. I mostly kept the marriage rite as I had read. I decided it would be my vow to Ethan on our wedding the day I read it. I spoke aloud in a soft, steady voice:

By our own hands in wedlock, I am crowned –
And now to be your woman I am found.
You are, you know, the only man for me.

Our dreams shall all be brought to life, you'll see.
On Planet Earth, our Terrain world of blue,
Our son will happily be with me and you.
Our daughter will be fair and quick of mind,
To many a Man, they will be good and kind.
By heaven, I am joined with you together,
You know I am your woman now forever.
The grandchildren we have will live afar –
We'll see them on that bright, distant star.

After we each proclaimed our love for one another, something fascinating happened to my perception of consciousness. I noticed that there seemed to be a vortex of energy behind the archway, in front of the vast Manitoba maple tree we had in our garden space. A vortex appeared to create an elemental portal between us both. Noticing this and breathing deeply, I recognised this sign from my angels and ancestors. This tremendous archetypal energy, I realised, would pave the way for generations to come. It would create a morphogenic field that would make it easier for our future children to tap into the true sanctity of marriage. It would not only allow us, but many others to tap into a space of love in nature more frequently. A sacred rite that had long been forgotten by many over the centuries.

We felt the momentum of the marriage rite as we merged together as one. The celebrations continued as everybody danced together around the fire pit. Everything we did on this day turned out to be so simple yet satisfying. This was primarily because we were connected to nature throughout the whole ceremony. We were related to this space of love, which we had previously nurtured. This gave the entire celebration even more meaning than we could have anticipated. It was the most important day of our lives!

Before the guests went home, we gave them little gifts of

native wildflower seeds to fit with the wild theme of our nature wedding. We wanted to promote the growth of Mother Nature as often as possible. By the evening time, I still felt a burst of energy running through me, even though I had only eaten a salad and some sugary wedding cake. To top off a most wonderful day, Ethan and I sat together in front of the fire pit. It was dark now, and everyone had disappeared. All that remained was the wedding arbour and the guests silver chairs that shone in the light of the full moon. We sat around the intimate fire with our bare feet placed on the rocks that formed the outside edge of the circle. I gazed at the moon and stars through the trees and felt a mystical energy present. It seemed as though time stood still for a moment as my thoughts completely emptied. I turned to face Ethan and felt a new wave of trust and love wash over my entire being. It felt so safe and comforted.

Throughout the whole day, I had repeated the mantra affirmations to myself:

I love you
I accept you
I respect you
I acknowledge you

This had helped me to stay present and positive with any social stress throughout the day. It helped elevate my sense of consciousness to be fully present throughout the whole day. Though, it had required a lot of energy to do so. Sat by the fire, my body suddenly began to channel some powerful energy from the elements—I could feel my entire being vibrating, and it took all of my attention to stay present to this occurrence.

I could almost hear the moon talking to me, whispering words of wisdom throughout this energy influx. The stars too seemed to be sending me downloads of information. I tried to breathe and ground into this overwhelming feeling. The elemental energy was extremely potent. So powerful that the following morning I could barely stay awake. I felt too tired and drained that I eventually had to take a nap, just hours after waking. Taking naps was something I rarely did. I realised though that I could not have asked for a more perfect wedding day. Even the stars had been congratulating us this night. We realised that we had both exerted a lot of upgraded energy on our wedding day, and even potentially changed our cellular body to its core. Love is a powerful, grounding force, indeed, but rest was required for both of us after this wonderful wedding.

THE CHRONICLES OF SYNCHRONICITY

SIXTEEN

The Journey To My Future Self

∞

It had been many moons since our sacred day. Even so, we were still full of the energy of our dreams. One cold, gloomy night, we decided to do another meditation ritual since the previous past life one had been so potent. This time focusing more on my future life and who I was going to become. After performing our ritual and getting into the relaxation body, I again visited the ancient home from my previous visitation. I was guided to climb up the stairs as opposed to down this time. I saw that these stairs ascending the house were made of a white crystal marble that spiralled much further beyond what my eyes could see. As I climbed the last step, two people greeted me from my soul star family group. They turned out to be the missing two who had not been inside the sun. I noticed that they were of a different species, and I had wondered about their origin, but felt too afraid to ask for some reason.

They proceeded to open mosaic looking doors with what looked like some kind of reiki channelling. I briefly noted their hand movements to be similar to the ones I had used before. These tall doors opened out onto a balcony, which overlooked a sizeable Elven kingdom. Before me, I could see and feel sublime waterfalls gently filling the air with a magical mist. The sounds of these rushing waters enveloped me completely. I could also see colourful towers that wrapped around trees seamlessly, all around.

Behind a pillar, a beautiful looking woman stepped forth. I noticed that she was a part humanoid part dolphin, and she could fly! She introduced herself to me and told me her name was Alina. She invited me to tour around her kingdom and I of course said yes. As we flew all throughout the realm, I saw lots of little stalls with people selling fresh produce. Alina swung to the right, and I noticed a gigantic, rainbow water fountain in the centre of the city. I smiled as I glimpsed lots of children who were playing in the area.

Alina spoke to me telepathically during this flight, telling me how I too was capable of creating and nurturing society, just like this. One that could live in total harmony with nature. She told me how she had been able to rise into her ranks. It had arisen out of her doing energy work with her mind and heart intelligence. Many years prior, they had come into balance within her being. She spoke to me of her past story and how she had come to be where she was today, a great queen of an elven kingdom.

Flying high and diving deep now, I did not feel any sense of vertigo, and in fact, enjoyed the trip immensely. Alina also spoke to me about a deep trust with life itself, and that everything in the world was related to our inner experience and interpretations. She shared so much wisdom with me that it was challenging to keep up. Next, we flew to an eastern corner of the city and Alina showed me a stone palace. It had luminous, mossy, green hair cascading the sides and crystals scattered within its walls. In front of the castle were lots of little faeries playing in the water and dancing around mushrooms. We finally landed at a table where many other elven kings and queens sat inside a bright tunnel. I realized that I was supposed to have a meeting with them regarding something, but I could not shake the feeling that it was time for me to leave.

Along with this thought, I instantly found myself back at my old home's secret garden. I felt somewhat disheartened that the experience had ended so suddenly, but decided that maybe I was not quite ready for what was to occur just yet. The most important lesson I learned during my time in viewing this future life visitation was that there was so much guidance and wisdom within, more than I could ever imagine. This elven kingdom was but a snapshot of what was to come for humanity I prophesied. I could not get enough of the fun I was having with these stories that played out in my mind, I had to explore more of my imaginal dreams whilst awake.

Later that same evening, I decided I wanted to play in my imagination again. I am greeted by Hathor once again and this time she tells me she wants to show me something. She proceeds to show me ancient Egypt and what it really looked like back then. I noticed that everything seemed much brighter within this vision of ancient Egypt. I realized it was because of some kind of mirror that seemed to cover many different buildings, including the pyramids. The light from these buildings reflected a dazzling central nature feature. This central feature was a long body of water with monuments, crystals and flora either side of black and white pillars. Along the edges of this were luscious trees and bushes, ripe for the picking. I looked over at Hathor and exclaimed how much more nature there seemed to be—more than what I had imagined.

Hathor motioned me over to a portal area at the end of this grandiose nature, water pathway. She told me I would be faced with a series of trials that I would have to overcome before I could reach the next stage of my consciousness. This involved integrating the conscious, subconscious, and most difficult of all, the unconscious shadows and fears of my being. To reach each area of my consciousness, I was going to have to tap into the different states of awareness, Beta, Alpha, and Theta. I suddenly remembered all of the dreams I had ever had in which I had been being tested somehow. They left as quickly as they had come to me, and I took this as a sign that I was indeed ready to face whatever was about to happen. My recent obstacle course dreams had been preparing me all along.

Quickly entering the portal, I could see another meeting taking place with The Founders, but a much older one in past times. Before i know it, I am seated, and they hand over to me a Lemurian crystal. They seem very cautious in telling me to utilize its energies only through the heart. The next moment we are on an island, and I am taken by surprise to see trees growing tall from the sand below. This forest beach, Hathor assures me, is where I will be greeted by in my dreams this night. I came around from the vision and realised that perhaps I would have to go even deeper into theta or delta state to know what she was talking about.

During a deep sleep that night, I was indeed greeted by a beach forest, but not in the way I had imagined. Instead, I was in Hobbiton, visiting an ancestor of mine. I knocked on her door but intuited to stand some feet away instead. It was nighttime, and the door did not open to greet me, instead, I noticed my ancestor was already sitting on the edge of a cliff just a few feet away. I walked over to her and told her that I could not sit down near such a long drop. She then proceeded to fill in space with high sand and trees sprung from underneath this new ground. I could even see native people in the distance which comforted me some. My ancestor told me I was going to go on a journey to let go and heal abandonment and rejection through my family line. I nodded, and before I could say anything else, I was galloping on a horse at light speed through nature. For a moment, I had no idea where I was and asked where I was going. Then, my whole body proceeded to shoot up into the sky. After some light speed flying through the air, I landed on another planet which looked similar to the moon.

Once there, I was greeted and stood before a circle of Egyptian Gods. All the while, I could hear a voice in my mind telling me to stand tall and be confident. I had some fear in me that felt like imposter syndrome and I started to wonder if these gods were going to reject me. Again, I heard the words of my ancestor whispering to me, telling me to remember my god self. Almost instantly, I willed myself to become the embodiment of the Egyptian goddess Hathor herself. As I released any fears of being noticed by these gods somehow, I felt myself become the entire essence of Hathor. I had passed the test, and now I was on to the next stage. I was suddenly transported to another area of the planet, and I sat kneeling and gazing at a humongous grey and pink moon in the sky before me. One of the Egyptian God's approached me, and I could sense my self readjusting my form and thoughts once more.

"What are you doing?" He inquired.

"I am prophesying with the moon" I replied confidently.

"I see, what about?" he pressed.

"About one of my future lives. I am explaining to the moon that I wish to carry the same traits as a goddess of love into a future life, but in a more subtle way." I share.

"And how will you do that?" he requested.

"By overcoming my fears of falling and stepping into the unknown," I reveal.

"And what does the goddess of love look like in your future incarnation?" He asks with interest.

With reflective confidence, I share, "it looks like my whole body turns into a pinkish rose colour as I am dancing and performing acrobatics seemlessly with others. The very essence of my love is my true purpose in action as future incarnation as 'Kate'. The deepest substance and feeling of love channels through my entire body and changes everyone that it touches. I have no need for prestige or status. Instead, I am entirely satisfied resting in my deepest feeling body of love."

"But how do you overcome your fears?" he asks, not knowing the answer for himself.

Just as soon as this Egyptian God asked me this question, I am suddenly bouncing high into the sky with a trampoline beneath my feet. I shortly reminisce into my current incarnation as Kate, who had always been afraid of heights. Now though, I was able to bring the wisdom of a previous life as Hathor to my lucid mind. I realized that this fear of falling had been passed down through my mother's line. Instead of fearing or cringing at each bounce on the trampoline, I surrendered entirely and then dove into the fall it even more. As I bounced high into the sky, time stood still as I waved at the moon and surrendered any fears I had about losing control of my body. Then, on the way back down, I placed my hands forwards and willed my body to follow the fall so that I could go even faster. It no longer felt like falling, but flying instead. I spent some time experiencing this euphoria and overcoming this fear within my body. Finally, I returned to my ancestor, who was sitting in the same spot I had left her in.

As I approached her, I once again noted her body language, it was firm yet somewhat standoffish. She did not face to greet me. Instead, she sat on the ground looking out into the distance. I sat down beside her and emulated her body language while asking, "Why does it seem like there is some distance between us?"

"You know who I am?" She asked.

"I'm not sure, but I think you have something to do with my Nan," I intuit.

"Yes, I am the one who orphaned her mother," she reveals.

All of a sudden, my whole body felt shocked and went into

a moment of fear. The many stories my Nan had ever told me about her mother flashed before my mind. I remembered how she explained her mother had been left to the care of some heartless nuns in an orphanage. After taking in the full realization of this deep wound within my female line, I gained my compsure again. I then looked at my third great grandma directly in the eyes and leaned in toward her forehead and placed mine to it. We both sat there forehead to forehead, and I put my hands together in a prayer position and said, "I forgive you. I carry no judgment towards you now."

"Thank you." She replied

"Thank you! You just helped me to overcome my fear of falling, I am so grateful to have met you here. Before I leave, is there anything else I can do for you?" I ask.

"Well, I am doing okay, but your great-grandma who is in-between lives is not doing so great, she is somewhat unwell," she reveals.

"Okay, perhaps I can come here another time to help?" I suggest.

Before she could say anything else, the dream ended. When I told Ethan about it the next morning, he suggested that the way I may be able to help could be here in the real world. He suggested that the act of unifying the family line through conversation with family members could help bring forward the perfect things to say to trigger a healing response. To deepen the dialogue, I got to looking into my family ancestry and figured out my third great grandma's name had also been Kate! The synchronicity felt wonderful.

I decided to give my Nan and Father a call that same week to see if I could find out more. After some in-depth talks, I was able to uncover who some of our ancestors had been. I was also able to uncover the roots of the deep pain associated with the stories they held onto and shared through the family tree. I was unsure if I had helped to heal anything or anyone in the process as yet, but I assumed time would tell.

THE JOURNEY TO MY FUTURE SELF

THE CHRONICLES OF SYNCHRONICITY

SEVENTEEN

Elemental Portals

∞

Around our town, there happened to be people who wanted to cut down more trees than ever to build upon the land. Some of these trees were hundreds of years old. We realized we had to step up to stop mass tree genocide currently occurring all over the planet. Rather than getting angry and frustrated by the current state of affairs, I channeled this energy by spending more time in nature. We were tired of complaining about the lack of care people had for the planet. Instead, we decided to give even more love toward our garden. This decision led to feeling even more peaceful within.

I knew these tests were part of us; somehow, they represented an errant paradigm that society still had towards nature. We used these trials and tribulations to stand up for what we believed in, especially amongst our close family. The technocracy was starting to take over in this current modern world. Artificial intelligence seemingly lured many people's focus away from the critical problems on our planet. Ethan and I believed in Original Intelligence (Nature) before letting any new app or device (dis) connect us to our humanity.

Spirit was calling me to the task. I decided to do a tree meditation and invited others to join me around the world. This tree meditation actually turned out to free my inner child. Knowing that many others across the world would be doing a tree meditation that same day made it even more special. This kind of intentional action by us all would change the morphogenetic field for generations to come. I will relay this tree meditation to you in detail.

Taking a moment to breathe into my body as I sat below the tree, I continued to send myself love in the same way I had done with our garden. I thought back to the previous evening when I had the instinct to use a prayer while I was pulling out various overgrown plants from our firepit. Most people call this 'weeding,' but I find that term to be equivalent to plant racism. Just because a particular plant is unwanted in an area, it doesn't deserve to be disrespected by a degenerative term like 'weed.' All plants have a name, a place, and a purpose, regardless of our personal opinion of them in our garden. I saw myself reliving this moment now, repeating a mantra with a smile on my face, the words:

I love you;
I'm sorry;
Please forgive me.
Thank you;
I love you;
Please forgive me.

One by one, the plants were gratefully responding to me. They accepted the fact that they were going to die as I pulled them. With the more attention I paid to each one, the easier the transition was for both of us. These plants were seemingly allowing my hands to easily pull them from out of the ground. Almost as though they were letting go and softly releasing their grip from the ground. Repeating this simple yet effective thank you prayer throughout, I could hear my angels and guides thanking me, as well as the plants themselves. They were grateful to simply be noticed as a living being, and I thought back to the many unconscious plant-pulling moments I had previously taken part in. I promised myself, and nature, to always be more vigilant of each and every life that I came into contact with.

I was adamant that this garden would be forever allowed to grow freely— for as long as we lived there in the very least. We had created many prayers and blessings within this garden, carefully placing crystals around the property and honouring the four corners. I now felt it my duty to protect all of this nature, and only did what was necessary when it came to pulling plants from the garden. The firepit was a sacred emblem to us, and we wanted the sand ring around its edges to be kept clear. Anyone who thought our garden should look aesthetically pleasing, over what function it served, would have an earful. I began explaining through online forums that instead of paying people to mow the grass all the time, we could plant wildflowers instead. These simple acts of kindness towards nature would actually benefit the ecosystem all around. No longer would people have to pay for so much grass cutting to take place. Not only this, but the beautiful flowers would attract things like the struggling local bee populations, butterfly's, and various little critters.

Since most people were too busy with the corporate world to care about nature, Ethan and I decided it would be our duty to teach this wisdom. It had been passed down to us by our pagan and native ancestors, helping us to realize the potential in allowing nature to grow. All of our neighbours were regularly using machines to cut their grass. Loud, intrusive sounds that could be heard from far away. In our garden, however, we let the grass grow. We left the leaves that fell stay right where they were whilst others collected them up to be sent away. We let the fallen leaves stay right where they were, primarily, because they provided such rich nutrition for the soil. We made a point to only plant more things in our garden as opposed to taking anything away from what was already naturally there. I felt so adamant that no one would get to touch our dear friends, including the plants and animals.

I repeated the same three-sentence prayer to myself now as I sank deeper and deeper into my body's relaxation during this meditation. I realised we were in the season of harvesting all of our intentions and goals set back in Spring. I decided I wanted to harvest the fruit of the seeds previously sown during this meditation. As I made this decision, an orange tree appeared before me in my vision. I breathed in the smell of this luscious fruit and took note of each orange. How plump, juicy and fragrant they were.

After spending some time gratifying the tree, I picked the nearest orange and spoke to it. Letting it know that I was about to eat and transform it through my own being. As I peeled the orange skins, I listened to the sounds intently. This gave me ASMR tingles all through my body. I began to feel into how amazing and blissful this orange would taste. Upon the first bite, a delectable sweetness poured onto my tongue, and I drank this delicious juice with pleasure. I savoured every single bite, and as I finished the last segment of orange, I noticed an elemental portal in the tree before me now. I knew it was an elemental portal because it had the shape of a door in its thick trunk, and every time I took a step closer, the door decreased in size.

I prepared myself to enter this portal by breathing deeply. Stepping closer, I noticed my whole being reduce in size as I entered through this intricate door. Inside was the most magnificent smells of orange and wood bark. I could feel every sense come alive in me, and my hands started to warm rapidly. I even explored movement and dance in my excitement. I caressed the edges of the walls. They were made of soft skin, similar to the inside of an orange. Then a rope hanging down the centre of the tree called to my attention. I began to climb up it without a second's hesitation, using all of my strength to do so. I did not feel scared, even as I looked down and remembered my fear of heights. Being inside of this tree felt incredibly nourishing and extremely mystical to me. I climbed so high that I could not believe my own strength, I realized that the orange had given me the extra zest I had needed to ascend so far.

Looking down now with a brief feeling of trepidation, I knew that I had to fall before I could fly. This simple notion had put my heart to rest. I realized now that if I were to fall, so too then would I fly. But I didn't fall. I reached the top of the tree and noticed that I was in a higher vibrational space now. It was gigantic up here, so many branches leading off into the heavens. Instead of fearing the unknown, I felt into the benevolence of the spirit that lived here. Everything became more prominent, bolder and more vivid as I stood atop this tree, taking in every element. As I looked above me, I saw that I was only a few inches between this dimension and the next. I decided to reach my hands up to the galaxy of stars above, displaying my gratitude and willingness to receive a message. Miraculously, I felt my hands being licked by a warm, wet tongue. I looked up with eager eyes to spot my cat friend. I laughed with joy at the remembrance of her preferred way to greet me.

Before I could say anything to my spirit animal, I glimpsed her opalescent, white wings in the distance swoop by. My dear lion friend now settled nearby, with a proud and majestic stance. I ran over to her, and we hugged and played together for a few moments. Apparently, she had summoned me here to go on a journey somewhere. So I climbed on her back and held on tight as

I knew she was going to take us on a ride. Soaring through the sky, flying as fast as the speed of light, I felt nothing but exhilaration throughout my whole body. We landed at our destination, and I saw that before me was a podium and two items. As I walked towards these two items, I sensed that I would have to choose one. Before me was a shining sword, and as I picked it up, I saw previous lifetimes of myself as a warrior through the mirror of its steel. I placed it back down, knowing that those days were hopefully behind me. My hands carefully reached for the second object. It was a crystal ball with shimmering, iridescent colours.

As I held this magical ball in my hands, I began to see myself within every other life that I had ever experienced as a high priestess. Holding this ball in my hands, my insides tingled as my DNA and cells imbued themselves with these memories. I felt my energy body expand ecstatically now. Every single emotion and triumph that I had ever experienced encapsulated me. Swiftly, I came back to my body and breath to keep my excitement from ending this meditation too quickly. There was a sense of eternity now pulsing through my veins. Instinctually I let the ball go, and as I did so, I noticed how it did not fall to the floor, but instead began to levitate around me. My feet suddenly hovered above the ground too, and I could feel my own body floating now. The crystal ball began to circle my entire auric field. Swirling and forming Celtic weaves and sacred geometry. My energetic body appreciated this new sense of spaciousness, and I relaxed into this feeling of expansion.

The crystal ball eased away from my body as it finished its final cycle of circling shapes. I sensed that its energy was a gift I received to take with me. I fell to my knees in gratitude for all the magnificent beings of light I could sense all around me. They had helped me throughout my life more than I could ever know. I wanted to hug each and every bright being of consciousness in this place. I watched the crystal ball transform into a diamond-like shape now. It was the exact same rounded diamond that had been with me since my awakening. It had many names, but I had long called it Evia. It was the colourful orb that I could not stop drawing and painting during my earlier days in falling in love with Ethan. Somehow his love had awoken this energy within me, and now it was going to become a permanent part of me. I watched as the orb came closer again, and its power merged with my own. My spine instantly straightened, and my body became almost weightless as its shape morphed with my stature. Synchronistically, it placed itself exactly where I had always imagined its presence emanating from.

I thought back to all of the times that I had ever needed to imagine its presence. These were mainly times during the night when I could feel malevolent energy in the room, or when I felt scared or nervous. I also had imagined the orb radiating out like a wave from my spine. It would appear at the click of my fingers, whenever I would feel afraid or needed some extra brightness within. Vibrating intense energies of protection and love. It had always been my stronghold. I walked ahead buoyantly within this vision now, and noticed a mirror before me. Staring into its reflection, I saw how powerful this light being orb was within my energy body. It was a multi-coloured iridescent crystal which carried all of my ancestral, angelic, akashic memory and knowledge. It was my higher self in light form, and it had always been my protector. I realized that this orb was my future self, trying to support me. This rainbow consciousness was actually alive with senses of its own. It was formed and sustained through love, it seemed.

It was my light body, in escrow, so to speak. It felt like a best friend to me.

The Evia light always had been there—even as a young child, but I had not know it at the time. I saw myself around the age of eleven in the mirror before me. It showed me that I had disconnected from it around this time during my teenage years. Now that I was more aware of its presence, I could not only see it but feel it. Even though my conscious mind did not know much about this presence, I knew it was a legacy. The mirror showed me how I could transform any situation or feeling in my being through the love this orb could channel within me. I looked overat my proud lion friend who stood tall, and strutted over to me. She watched closely in the mirror, just as a best friend would, protective yet nurturing.

I saw white energy emanating from behind my shoulders now, and noticed some transparent ivory wings had amazingly appeared. They slowly began to unfurl from behind my back. My body felt a jolt of majesty, purity and grace run through it. The feeling was incredible, the beauty of these visions continued to increase. I held onto my heart with both of my hands now as I realized how grateful I was. I had a glittering, grandiose remembrance of who I really was at my soul core. My lion friend addressed me now and told me it was time to leave. I climbed aboard her back, and she instantly swooped low and soared high, quickly carrying us through the air. I began to softly sing as we flew back home to thank this vision. I wanted to share my songs of praise for having experienced this unbelievable place of victory and freedom.

I hugged my spirit animal goodbye, and she intently warned about future moments to come. I probed her for more information, but she told me not to worry. Instead, this orb had been gifted to me for a reason. She reminded me that I would face many trials and tribulations and would need to call upon my power, love, and strength as often as possible. I nodded and felt tingles on the insides of my head, almost instilling a sense of knowing. I knew that I had a grander calling in this life, and I felt ready for all of it.

I slowly came back down to reality and shifted into the waking world. I woke up with a massive headache in the centre of my brow. I asked for help with this pain as I was unsure of the source. The area had been feeling tense and painful for many days prior. I simply shook it off, intuiting that perhaps all the profound downloads I was receiving were moving too expeditiously for my brain to process all at once. Even with this migraine, I still felt I was floating somehow. Almost as though I had physically gone to this ethereal world during my tree meditation. As I relaxed into this feeling, I noticed that this simple call for aid was about to be answered in my waking world. I sensed my angels were now in front of my view, though I couldn't see them with my physical eyes. Something started to tap and touch different areas of my forehead, and energetically I could feel it moving around the energy inside of my head. The pain began to lessen, and I could feel my headache and tension begin to subside.

I quietly thanked this being in my mind and again saw myself hugging them. It felt as though I had woken up to my own love. I jumped for joy as I stood tall now. I was beginning to feel and taste the flavours of my real being, and it was delicious! During this profound meditation, I had learnt to establish rules with myself. Rules that whenever I felt any form of pain body arise in me, I would acknowledge these feelings completely. Then I would remember my effervescent energy body encapsulated by this crystal orb. I already knew that by practising this acceptance and remembrance would entail a significant improvement in being able to cope with any situation. I used the prayer that nature had inspired within me. It was like poetry that I kept repeating to myself and to everything and everyone else:

I love you;
I acknowledge you;
I respect you;
Thank you.

EIGHTEEN

A Light Story of Humanity

∞

Over the next few months, Ethan and I had synchronistically come across sources spurning our interest in visionary hypnosis. I finally realized that the visions I had been having for most of my life were of great value to me and many others. It seemed I had been in similar brain wave states as clients had under hypnosis. Because of my innate ability to go inward in this way, we thought it was about time to start taking it more seriously. With Autumn now over, I had already experienced several mysteriously magical visitations from my ancestors, due to the thinning of the veil around Halloween. I knew that I could go anywhere during these journeys, all I had to do was set the intention. Ethan had started to learn more about hypnosis so that he could guide me and talk to me whilst I was in this trance-like alpha-brain state.

Hypnosis, it appears, is not like what they portray on TV. It's not some silly person in a coat and hat putting people to sleep and making them do all sorts of ridiculous things. This is overhyped stage-show stuff. It's actually quite the opposite. Actual hypnosis, and its therapeutic capability, involves taking people into clearly focussed places of consciousness. This is happening in full awareness, not in some sleepily vulnerable state of hypersuggestibility. Hypnotherapy can help direct us into a state of hyper-consciousness that allows us to experience all kinds of heightened states of awareness—including experiencing past lives, ancestral realms, and even our life between physical incarnations.

One particularly clear night, I stepped outside into the snow to be met with a beautiful crescent moon and array of stars. I breathed into their celestial beauty and shouted up to Ethan that he ought to come look before bed. The previous few nights had been rainy and cloudy. So I took every opportunity I could to spend time with the celestial bodies when they appeared. I grabbed my camera and knelt down to take pictures of the moon. They turned out blurry so Ethan got the binoculars instead, and we both gazed upon the stars and moon up close. It was such a delight to be able to see the real moon and not just a picture on a screen. The plasma that reflected from the moon and shone from the stars fed my soul. Just after I pulled the binoculars away, I noticed five grey looking doves flying together in the night sky. I quickly pointed this out to Ethan, but by the time his eyes reached to the source, they had disappeared.

"Woah, I just saw what looked like five grey birds flying in-synch, completely disappear into the sky," I gasped.

"Well, they could've disappeared behind a cloud?" Ethan said.

"I see absolutely no clouds in sight whatsoever. Look for yourself, do you see any clouds?" I asked.

"No, I don't, but maybe it was an aeroplane. Or maybe even a UFO," Ethan said sarcastically.

"I'm telling you I saw what looked like five birds in the sky and they disappeared into thin air. I've never seen white/grey looking birds in the late-night sky like that," I proclaim.

"I have," Ethan recalls.

"When?" I retorted.

"During the night when I used to cycle home in Saskatchewan," he reflects.

"Well maybe you saw the same thing, but you didn't keep your eyes on them long enough to notice that they disappeared into thin air?" I asked inquiringly.

"Maybe," Ethan shrugged. "Usually my eyes do this jerky-movement-thing and then whatever was there quickly blends into the night sky again."

"I don't know what that was, but it felt mystical. When I think of looking up into the sky and seeing things, usually the idea of lights of ships comes to mind. But that always seems so invasive. But this... This felt special, like seeing some kind of angel birds disappearing into a sky portal."

We stepped inside after feeling exceptionally grateful to connect with the elements, not saying another word about the birds. Once I had finished brushing my teeth, I heard subtle drumming coming from the bedroom. I walked over to the bed to find Ethan tapping our new drum.

He smiled and asked, "Ready for another journey?"

"Yes!" I replied gleefully.

I climbed on top of the covers and used a small blanket to keep me warm. Ethan asked me where or what I wanted to do this time.

"I want to go into our future," I replied confidently.

"Into our future secret garden, it is," smiled Ethan.

I closed my eyes now as Ethan reminded me to breathe. Using his new skills as a hypnotherapist, he had stopped tapping on the drum and focused on me. As Ethan is my husband—not someone I pay to see as a professional hypnotherapist—he chose to begin gently stroking my open hand to help induce a state of relaxed trance, something I found deeply comforting. As he began to coach me into a relaxing space, I completely allowed my mind to empty. As I did this, I noticed how my usual auto-pilot thoughts were suddenly silent. Lying on the bed, allowing my body to relax, I realized how all too often I got caught up in the story of my thoughts. Now though, I was going somewhere, and I was determined to focus on my breath and listen to Ethan's guiding voice.

It took no longer than five minutes for me to be able to see some lush greenery and be immersed in nature. As I tried to breathe into this space, Ethan asked me, "How does your body feel. How's your breathing?"

"Steady" I replied.

"Good, so now I want you to imagine our secret garden, can you do that?" Ethan asked.

"I see a Fairy Forest. I'm there right now" I replied.

"Oh okay, and what do you see in this Fairy forest?" Ethan requests.

"I can see and smell many tall trees, and I can hear water nearby." I reveal.

"What are you doing in this forest?" he guides.

"I'm collecting water and to giving a gift of gratitude to the elements that live here," I share.

"What is this water for?" Ethan asks.

"It is crystal clear water for us to drink. I am bringing it to our home," I note.

"Is it clean and refreshing?" Ethan requests.

"Yes, the purest water I've ever drank before. Now I am laying some corn and an apple on the ground," I share as I experience a wondrous scene unfolding.

"What are these for?" He asks.

"They are from our garden. These are our gifts to the elements and the fairies for giving in abundance and allowing us to be here," I share.

Next, I explain to Ethan that I am walking back slowly through these woods, following a pathway that leads to our secret garden. He asks me softly yet excitedly what our yard looks like. I tell him that the garden is distinct from the forest. It is spacious and splendidly quaint. Stepping up the path, the hill leads to long grass and wildflowers all around. There are many mini areas all throughout the garden, which compose of different intentions and uses for us. I explain that I can see one area inside of the wildflower grass that holds a natural pond with fishes and frogs. In another area of the garden, I can see a walkable maze that the children often like to play games in. I begin approaching the house now. As I do, I am greeted by the future Ethan in my vision. We stroll towards the other part of the garden, which comprises of our freshly grown food. Ethan walks past me into the salad and herb garden, picking our meals for the day while I stay back and pick luscious fruits from the tree garden just in front.

Note: for editorial simplicity, I will use our initials for this part of the dialogue. I will be K, and Ethan, E.

E: "How old am I in this vision?"

K: "About fifty. You have quite a few silver hairs about you."

E: "What about our children?"

K: "Elle is running over to show me a butterfly that landed on her finger. She is around five or six years old."

E: "And do we have a son?"

K: "Yes, we do. Our son is older and is playing with the fish in the pond."

E: "I see, so what are we doing now?"

K: "We are discussing what we are going to have for breakfast and lunch. The children and I are agreeing on a fruit salad for breakfast, and we sit nearby our bird table to eat our breakfast together."

E: "I see. What kind of birds are at the bird table?"

K: "I can see some chickadees and some cardinals just now. I am also asking our son to go and fetch some sweet potatoes after breakfast. He sighs as he wanted to go and explore in the forest instead."

...Pause. After a few moments of allowing me to immerse myself more fully, Ethan began again:

E: "What's happening now?"

K: "Now you are headed to the kitchen. I am going to the chicken dens with Elle who asks to come with me."

E: "What does our kitchen look like?"

K: "It is very rustic yet modern-looking. Lots of wood and, bright, open soace. There are three windows, all of which you can see out into the garden."

E: "I bet I still have my trusted knife with me?" Ethan jokes.

K: "Yes, you do, and now you are chopping some vegetables, listening to mine and Elle's conversation." I reply, smugly.

E: "What are you saying?"

K: "Our daughter is asking me if we can camp out this night. I tell her tomorrow we can instead as we have to do something special tonight."

E: "And what about our social life, what does it look like during this time?"

K: "We have a cosy yurt where we hold most of our socializing sessions with people. We play music together and create sacred space around the fire. We share and express ourselves as a close group. Everyone contributes to these gatherings because it brings so much value to their lives. I also have weekly yoga and meditation classes in the morning. These are held in the garden or in our greenhouse."

Then Ethan asks me to jump forward into the following nighttime. He begins leading me into the forest to perform a special ritual of some kind. I interrupt Ethan halfway through this guided visualization and tell him that I cannot leave our children alone in the house. He agrees, and instead, I begin to share with him the unique space we have created for this instead. It happens to already be in our garden. As I walk towards this space, I can see an archway that leads into a hanging bench. Though it is dark, fairy lights guide my way. I sit upon this swinging bench now, and I tell Ethan I can see a crystal orb in front of me. This orb is shimmering brightly with the reflection of the full moon.

Just then I realize what the 'special' plan had been that meant we could not camp out this night. It occurs to me that this is a special night celestially and seasonally, we have prepared for this moment to come. We set this sacred space to honour the elementals at twilight. Ethan then asks me what the crystal orb is for, and I tell him it is for both my knowing and my exploring. The wind is still. The air is silent. All I can sense is the very presence of Spirit with me now as I gaze into the glowing crystal.

E: "What is happening?"

K: "Right now, I am placing a moonflower next to the crystal orb, offering a gift of gratitude to the Ethers."

E: "What are you doing with this orb?"

K: "It is a quartz crystal of some kind, and I am using it to consult my inner oracle and receive advice and messages from the beyond."

E: "What kind of messages do you receive?"

K: "I am being shown how to help our children with some of the problems they face. I am also being shown what to teach the people that come to our community every week."

Ethan allows for a short pause to deepen the experience further.

E: "Are we happy in this life?"

K: "Yes, we are delighted and have an abundance of gifts from the universe. We really have everything and more that we could have ever asked for. Though now it's getting late, and I best be getting to bed."

E: "Okay, so now you are going back to the house?"

K: "Yes," I reply, calmly.

Pause while Ethan continues to talk, but my attention is completely taken by something else.

E: "What is it?"

K: "I just saw a lost witch trying to visit my daughter in her dream."

E: "You mean, she tried to talk to her while she is asleep?"

K: "Yes. This lost witch is gone now, though. As soon as she senses my presence, she cannot stick around. I am going to perform a protection spell before we go into the house."

E: "What does she want with our daughter?"

K: "She waits around the forest for her own children, who left many years ago. She tried to be a good mother to them, but she became weak and gave into anger. I don't know the full story, all I know is that she keeps trying to lure our daughter away so that she can feel like a mother again. She is some kind of reflection of my own darkness which I could fall into if I ever became complacent"

E: "But you won't let that happen?"

K: "Never. Dark forces have no power here, and they know it. I can see beyond the witches follies and see that she is a lesson for us. One that reminds us to never stray from the path of truth. She will never be able to get to our daughter, so long as our daughter stays true to herself."

E: "But you are afraid?" Ethan senses.

K: "I have always been afraid. For as long as I can remember, these inherent gifts of mine have come with so-called downfalls. This is not the first time I have seen this witch, and it won't be the last until she can go to the light."

E: "What about your protection spell, will it work?"

K: "Yes, it helps. The doors and windows to the house are locked, but there is nothing anyone can do to keep the lost witches away. They come because of the abundance of love that is here. Seeking to steal their own share of it."

Note: Ethan later shared with me that before I began speaking about the witch, he saw her sort of 'jump' out of my mind toward him, something akin to what he saw when we were experiencing Ayahuasca.

After a pause for some deepening, Ethan continues:

E: "What are you doing now?"

K: "I am in our daughter's bedroom, directly opposite to our son's bedroom. I kiss her on the forehead and smile at her beautiful resting face. I stop briefly on the way out to our bedroom to watch you tucking in our son, who is fast asleep too."

E: "Okay, if you were to bring back the feeling of this future vision to the present moment, what would it feel like?"

K: "Steady but with extra love," I sighed joyfully.

After cleansing the whole house and muttering protections of Light Language, I climb into bed with future Ethan by my side. Ethan falls asleep within minutes, and I hold his hand in mine while staring out of our bedroom ceiling windows. I recognise the feeling of being wholly contented and fulfilled by life as I gaze at the stars. I have so much energy that some days I simply don't even know what to do with it. At the same time, with all of this knowledge and wisdom within my future, there comes great responsibility.

While laying still in bed now, I begin to think about how this lost witch is really here to show and teach me responsibility. I have nothing to learn from her behaviours as a person, but her soul's intrusions teach me valuable lessons about what it means to 'have it all.' No matter how many locks my home has, no matter how strong and confident I am as a woman, there is always the potential to have something taken from me. Instead of worrying about this, I decided that staying true to my path will always lead me to where I want to go. I simply have to surrender to this lack of control, knowing that my life is also in the hands of God.

I eventually fall asleep within the vision and have dreams of trying to keep the witch out. Every single time though, I can overcome her. With the golden rays of the sun peeking through our window, I am wide awake again in the vision. I kiss Ethan a good morning and step outside to perform my daily routine of collecting water. On the way, I gaze towards the horizon, where the sunrise is just high enough to cast its rainbow rays upon the land. I fall to my knees in gratitude for this great life and for this extraordinary space of love. All from our garden, we can watch the sunrise as well as the moonset. I feel overwhelmed in the best possible sense, with both gratitude and mystification. Ethan slowly guides me back to the present moment now. Ushering me out of this vision by bringing my awareness into my body. I wiggle my toes and fingers as I open my eyes. Ethan and I smile at each other and fall sound asleep shortly after.

...

To end this book is also to start a new journey. Kate and Ethan continue to dream their precious dreams forward. Although these dreams are already real. Time is an illusion. Both the past and future exist simultaneously. So in the spirit of now and what is possible, let me take you to another future scenario.

One day, while working in their garden, another elemental portal opens up. Not through meditation, but in real life. Out of it steps a Lemurian Lyrian, looking exceptionally similar to us humans, if it were not for the distinguishable glow around its body. This Lyrian greets and welcomes Kate and Ethan to venture into the between world. Ethan and Kate had finally figured out how to open Elemental Portals together, and their friend had been waiting for the right opportunity to invite them when no other neighbours were around. This in-between space bridged the gap between the material and spiritual world.

As they enter this place, it is blue and has invisible paths leading to individual nature bubbles. These nature bubbles are different places scattered across both Earth and other planets. The trails there are only visible when the light of the sun shines on them in a certain way and reveals irredescence along its edges. This Lyrian tells us that we can use this space to visit any place in nature we want. As an exchange, Kate is needed to attend special meetings with galactic and ancient councils that take part in the synchronicity chronicles beyond time. These are expeditions which help planets like Earth to ascend into higher consciousness. They begin visiting a world named Tirea, which is similar to Earth. Together, Kate and Ethan go there through astral travel and take part in an ardent training process.

The idea and notion of connecting with their galactic heritage and family become the single most interesting, exciting, and fascinating potential discovery. To meet their galactic brothers and sisters is an exhilarating idea for them indeed. They attend meetings with future humans who have already ascended into light beings. We regularly discuss how we can bring these teachings back down to earth, to aid in the enlightenment of the material planet.

We learn so much during our time spent within this in-between world. Including the notion that no one knows what we are really capable of. We are to remember that everything we can imagine is real. Throughout these experiences, Kate comes across a long lost brother in the spirit realm. He is the guardian over a planetary consciousness, and his powers involve using light energy to create cities and solar bodies for his people. Kate and Ethan see that one day they will evolve to this level too. They also see that the future of humanity is unravelling for the highest good of all. Especially once humans delve deeper into the cosmic mysteries of our times.

We collectively begin preparing for a new planet, a 'New Earth' so to speak. Planet Tirea is basically a blueprint baby earth. To qualify for this new planet, we have to go through lots of challenging training. Our dreams begin to be filled with lots of obstacle courses and challenging scenarios to overcome. It is the most testing training we have ever been through, emotionally, spiritually, and physically. But we are tested in this way because we have acquired all of the tools necessary to accomplish such tasks.

After all of this hard work, we continue smiling through the difficult times. The life of our dreams becomes so real that it is more than we could have ever asked for. A real possibility to bridge the two worlds harmoniously comes together. Eventually, the spirit world becomes merged with the physical world. People begin living from their hearts in balance with their minds. This creates a whole new reality, involving all necessary parts for the truth to emerge. Elemental portals become teleportation spots that allow us to collectively travel wherever we desire in nature. We begin to believe in adventuring beyond our wildest dreams.

Life then starts to make a lot more sense. Day by day, we begin to understand more of our past, and where we are headed in the future. Many of the final pieces of the puzzle come together. A euphoric elation comes about within our civilisation when the majority realize that life is an infinite dance! Souls begin remembering their eternal nature and start to usher in the new generation of love. Synchronisitcally, the tapestry of our lives, had been being woven all along. Only now did we entirely recognize our full potential in all of it. We accept and finally understand that we are divine beings, and all that we need is here in this moment right now.

We have been, and will always be, on a path of ever-increasing enlightenment and ever-expanding ascension. Our soul is on a journey through life which ultimately seeks to end all suffering. We realize that we are the medicine, and that life is the ritual. As we begin getting close to ascending to the next level, we can use our higher gifts. Skills such as telepathy, clairsentience, telekinesis, and clairaudience are free for all to use—all of which arise out of deep empathy and sensitivity. At the beginning of our lives, this sensitivity seemed like a hindrance or maybe even a curse. Now we see that it was a dormant ability just waiting to be used to its full potential. This sensitivity allows us to see and feel things in the world as they indeed are.

This leads us to be able to have a greater understanding of our everyday lives, too. Finding the magic in both the mundane and the arcane—in the micro-moments as well as the macro ones. We continually communicate with our galactic brothers and sisters as well as with the elementals and mother nature. All based on a balanced resonance and reverence for life that we now hold as a collective. Understanding our real history from this more profound connection to life, we are informed of the true Light Story and history of our planet.

The real Light Story of humanity is one that helps us to realize everything has always been for the highest good of all. Yes, we have all made mistakes. But from each, we've grown exponentially more than we could have imagined. As seen from Source, everything, even war and violence, is simply another shade of love. However, we must all wisely choose what to do with the time that is given to us. Then simply stay on the path that our soul knew before stepping into this body.

All along, the darkness and shadow stories have been a crucial part of our expansion. These common, collective, past mistakes have helped to bring us more clarity during this journey through life. In their presence, more light can unfold because of the very nature of this reflective, dualistic universe. They have a ripple effect on all of consciousness. No one can do anything to another, without first doing it to themselves. And so we finally recognize that we are all indeed connected. To everything. When we use our senses wisely, without attaching judgement, we can become aware of the silent presence of All.

We acknowledge all beings as part of Source, and allow everything that is within us to be recognized outside of us as well. As above so below. Through this life-source we inhabit as souls, we have been entrusted an ancient gift. It's been passed on by generations of ancestors, knowingly or unknowingly. This gift allows us to breathe at the apex of an infinite spiral—opening fully to the vision of the future. We come to terms with our own shadows by surrendering to what is and are reunited with our pure light being Self. This gift—a sacrosanct seed, of sorts—is the sacred merging of the spirit world and the physical world together as one. We, as inheritors of this wondrous gift, are the holy child—sovereign, free to experience all that this existence has to offer and learn how to be evermore saintly as we grow.

If we can allow Spirit every single day to be a central pivot of our expression, we can remember who we really are. This does not mean that the challenges we face will be comfortable in life. But they will always help us to grow, and won't feel so impossible to overcome after all. Both light and dark are like friends who are nervous about meeting again—perhaps even scared of the stark contrast in perspective. But once seen for what they really are, only Self is left to bear witness. And this Self is just trying to point us in the direction of our pure heart. All is Self.

Our whole existence has become fragmented from Source for a reason. Without this experience, humans would not have learned as much about who we are as we have so far. We chose to come to Earth to learn more about ourselves. Realtime, present expression in the now-ness of it all, is entirely new and sacred. This is the purpose of Life, to know more about ourselves than we ever did before. To gain a vaster understanding of all that we are, through every current of our individual and collective expression. Within every light and shadow of our existence. We each previously agreed to understand the Whole by first understanding our own selves in this life.

Everything is perfectly designed throughout karmic time and space. All is understood and learned from through micro and macro moments in time. Everything really is quite as beautiful as it could ever be. Eventually, when it comes to our own time to pass on into the spirit world, our children will carry this message on for us, and keep the true sanctity of life alive and thriving in wonderful ways. They will always have the ability to do an even better job than us, thanks to our own healing work before them.

Several cycles down the line, many of us will come back to this new planet that we have set in motion. We will live amongst this harmony, peace and truth. That which we dreamed into existence and continually intended for in lives previous. We rejoice in the infinite bounteousness of this life, in all of its forms. We do this by tapping into the unconditional love for all beings, right here, right now.

Your life is not what you think it is. You are a wondrous living harmony of the Elementals, your Soul, and Karma—all of which lives through you, as you. Your Quest, if you choose to accept it, is to innerstand your opportunities and responsibilities that branch out into infinity when fully adorned.

One final notion I will leave you with is the age-old adage, "Before enlightenment, chop wood and carry water. After enlightenment, chop wood and carry water." This stays relevant and revelatory to Kate and Ethan in the years to come. They continue to live healthy lives but always seek the magic within the mundane. Ethan progresses in his studies with hypnotherapy while Kate advances in her travels to in-between worlds. They continue to uncover all sorts of prized information about ancestors, angels, and the overall archetypes that govern our lives as human beings.

To be continued...

www.ingramcontent.com/pod-product-compliance
Lightning Source LLC
Chambersburg PA
CBHW020904080526
44589CB00011B/439